Hidden Paths
&
Secret Gates

Best Wishes
from
Kirstin E⸺

Two roads diverged in a wood, and I –
I took the one less travelled by,
And that has made all the difference.

(*from* The Road Not Taken *by Robert Frost*)

Hidden Paths
& Secret Gates

Six all-day walks around Bath

Still round the corner there may wait
A new road or a secret gate,
And though we pass them by today,
Tomorrow we may come this way
And take the hidden paths that run
Towards the moon or to the Sun.

(*from* The Lord of the Rings *by J.R.R. Tolkien*)

Kirsten Elliott & David Purchase

Millstream Books

Acknowledgements

Thanks are due to the following: staff at Somerset, Wiltshire and Bath Record Offices; staff at Bath Reference Library and at the Local History section of Wiltshire Reference Library; the librarian at Box Library; Lesley Freke at Wiltshire County Council's Archaeological Department; Rob Bell and Marek Lewcun of Bath Archaeological Trust; Anna McIlwaine at the Royal Air Force Museum; staff at Forest Enterprise; Footpath Officers at Somerset, Wiltshire and former Avon County Councils. We must thank Mrs Monica Bradley for her reminiscences of Biddestone, Mr & Mrs Sudbury for help and information in the Box Area, and Peter Warren for material about Limpley Stoke and Freshford. We would also like to thank the landlords who provided information about their pubs and the various members of the public who were ready to chat about their local area. Finally, as readers will detect, we derived a great deal of information from church guide-books. All too often the authors of these are anonymous, but we hope they and their families will accept our grateful thanks for supplying what is often a source of local as well as church history.

However, this book is dedicated to the Bristol Actuarial Society Walking Club. At one time or another the members have participated in all of these walks, often in some very interesting conditions, as well as providing inspiration for some of the routes. Without their help, friendship, insults, puns and astonishing ability to eat sticky puddings, this book might not have been written.

First published 1996 by
Millstream Books, 18 The Tyning, Bath BA2 6AL

© Kirsten Elliott and David Purchase 1996
ISBN 0948975415

This book is set in 10 point Palatino and printed in Great Britain by The Matthews Wright Press, 52 Furnham Road, Chard, Somerset

Contents

Introduction

In this book we describe six 'all-day' walks in the country within easy reach of Bath. In selecting walks to recommend to you, we have naturally tried to ensure that all the walking is of high quality, and that there is plenty of variety within each one. But we have also kept the following needs in mind.

We know that many walkers do want to go out for a day, and not just for two or three hours. But as a corollary, a suitable pub that is reached at lunchtime is a 'must'. All but one of these walks are between 11 and 13 miles long; the exception is 16$\frac{1}{4}$ miles, though it is on easy, open country (and we give details of a short cut which can be used near the end, if necessary - as we do for other walks where practicable). All are within 25 miles of Bath, by road. And all are south of the M4; for to the north, the Cotswolds are well covered by books of all shapes and sizes (and, dare we say, qualities).

One chapter covers each walk. We have tried to give a full route description (*in italics*) so that you should be able to follow the walk without a map if necessary. Our object in giving so much detail is to enable you, except at tricky points, to find the route without having to refer to the book all the time. You should be enjoying the scenery! We have also given much information about the places of interest that you pass, or see during the walk, in order to increase your enjoyment of the day.

It is likely that, as a reader of this book, you have some experience of walking in the country; so we do not presume to give elementary instructions. However, we do suggest that, even if you are a very experienced walker, you read the rest of this introduction before setting out, as there are a number of simple conventions that we use and describe, as well as some advice, for example about timing for the pubs. At the end of the introduction there is a table which summarises information about the six walks, to help you to choose which one to do next.

Directions

Throughout the book, the directions that you need to follow in order to complete the walk are given in *italics*. Text in roman type (like this) provides information about points of interest that you will pass. Text that is indented from the margins will normally refer to alternative routes (such as short cuts).

One of the most difficult aspects of describing walks such as those in this book relates to changes of direction. It would be unlikely to be helpful, and certainly tedious in the extreme to give compass bearings! We have therefore adopted a number of conventions which we hope will enable you to follow the routes without difficulty; these are summarised here.

○ When you have to turn left or right, we abbreviate the direction to 'L' or 'R'. But when we are giving additional information (e.g.'Keep the trees on your right') then 'left' or 'right' is spelt out.

○ We usually mention all significant changes of direction. However, if you are following a clear track or path, with no junctions, then we do not always draw attention to changes unless they are corners.

○ The phrase 'turn R' (or L) implies that you should turn through 90° or thereabouts. 'Bear R' means that you should change direction by less than 90°; 'veer R' suggests quite a small change of direction. 'Turn sharp R' is used on those rare occasions when you have to turn through more than 90°, almost doubling back.

○ 'Straight ahead' or 'on the same line' means that you continue in the same direction that you have been following. 'Straight across' (a field) means that you walk at right angles away from the hedge or fence behind you.

○ When we refer to a 'T-junction' you will approach along the 'leg' of the T, so that you have to turn either L or R: and similarly for a 'Y-junction'.

○ In the route descriptions, a 'road' or a 'lane' will denote a surfaced road unless clearly indicated otherwise (e.g. a 'green lane' is an unsurfaced ancient trackway). We do not imply that the road is a public one; it may be a private road which is a Right of Way as a footpath. (There is more on Rights of Way later.) A 'track' is unsurfaced, but wide enough for use by a farm vehicle such as a Landrover. A 'path' is less wide and mainly suitable for walkers; sometimes it may be open to horse-riders also, and a few are used by cyclists, but we do not distinguish between these.

○ Lastly, when we mention a gate or stile, you should assume that you go through or over it unless the description clearly indicates otherwise. However you should not assume that we mention every gate and stile, especially on fairly long and otherwise straightforward stretches.

In concluding this section we will emphasise what may well be obvious - that things change! Indeed during the year or so when we were writing this book, there were two or three alterations in each walk as a result of changes on the ground. So if you come to a point where the route description does not seem to 'fit', then think about whether this could be as a result of such a change. Sometimes it may be fairly obvious, e.g. if you find a brand-new gate where we refer to an old stile. On other occasions you may not be so sure; but if the rest of the route seems right, and you are confident that you have not strayed from the intended line, then a change is quite likely. Partly because of the possibility of these changes, we have often included information in the descriptions which is not needed to find the route, but which serves as a useful confirmation that you are indeed still on the right path.

Distances

We have quoted, in the details for each walk, the total distance covered. In the text describing the routes we indicate distances to some of the key points, measuring distances from the start for the morning walk, and from the lunch stop for the afternoon walk.

Distances are given in both metric and imperial units, and the abbreviations 'km' and 'm' are used for kilometres and metres respectively. We have given the metric units first because, for those using Ordnance Survey maps, it is easy to estimate metric distances 'by eye' using the grid squares which are at 1 km (1,000m) intervals. For relatively short distances (less than 800m or half a mile), however, we give values in metres only because for all practical purposes the distance in yards is the same. If you want to be supremely accurate you can add 10% - but can you really tell the difference while you are walking along between, say, 300 yards and 330 yards? Not many walkers carry a tape-measure with them!

We frequently give fairly short distances, for example from one path junction to the next. You do not need to concentrate on these. But in our experience, descriptions that lack this information can be worrying. If we are told to 'walk until you reach a path branching off to the right', after 5 minutes or so we begin to wonder if we have gone past the junction without noticing it (quite easy to do, if there are several in your group, chatting away!). By noting the distances, which you can use to estimate rough times as described in the next section, you will probably find it easier to concentrate on the surrounding country without worrying all the time about the route.

Times

There are real dangers in giving estimated times for walks, as everyone has a different pace. A time which may appear generous to one walker will seem much too fast to another. Nevertheless most people would like some idea of how long a walk may be expected to take, and we have therefore given some estimates in this book. We hope that they are at least reasonably consistent with each other, so that if you, having done one walk, find (for example) that you took only 80% of our suggested time then you will probably find that you complete other walks correspondingly faster as well. You may also find the estimates useful in deciding whether there is time to complete the full walk, or whether a short cut would be desirable.

Our intention is that these estimates are reasonably generous, bearing in mind that you may have to pause from time to time to check that you are correctly following the route. We have accordingly based them on a walking speed of about $3\frac{1}{2}$ km ($2\frac{1}{4}$ miles) an hour, with some adjustments for the terrain and for any hills. But they will not, of course, allow for any long rests that you may have, or time spent on photography or studying in detail the features that you pass. As with the distances, we have given times from the start or from the lunch stop, as appropriate. You must decide for yourself how long you want to spend over lunch, and add that to the total time.

For short distances you could assume, as examples, that 100m will take under 2 minutes, 250m about 4 minutes, 300m about 5 minutes and 400m about 7 minutes.

If you are in a group of any size, bear in mind that the larger the party, the slower the progress. This is especially true when (as on many of these walks) there are plenty of stiles to cross.

Pubs

In deciding on the walks to recommend, an essential feature was a suitable pub for lunch. We have tried so to arrange things that you reach the pub before the half-way point of the walk, as for many people too early a start is not welcome, whereas they are happy for the afternoon to be rather longer; however this has not always proved possible.

We have ourselves visited all the pubs mentioned and been very happy with the lunches and snacks available. However things can change, both for better and for worse. If you want to be on the safe side you could phone the pub beforehand to check that it is still open and serving meals at lunchtime on the day you are doing the walk.

(We certainly recommend phoning in advance if you are walking in a group of more than six people.)

One word of warning. Many of these pubs are very popular, especially at weekends and in the summer. If you do not want to be delayed too much at lunchtime it would be wise to plan to reach the pub fairly early - say, before 12.30 p.m. - another reason why we have tried to ensure that the pub is reached before half-way. (Most of the pubs will start serving lunchtime food at noon but you may find one or two that do not start until 12.30 p.m.)

For those of you using Ordnance Survey maps (see next section), we mention that in some cases the map does not mark the actual position of the pub very accurately. The symbol 'PH' will correctly show that there is (or was) a pub in the village, but not necessarily precisely where. So take note of our description of how to find your lunch stop.

Maps

We have written the route descriptions in sufficient detail that you should not need any maps other than the sketch maps included in this book. However, many walkers prefer to carry the appropriate Ordnance Survey ('OS') map at all times, and we would certainly agree that this can be helpful, not only for finding the route but also to identify objects and places that are seen on the way. In the details for each walk we have therefore given the relevant sheet numbers, for both the 1:50,000 (Landranger) and the 1:25,000 (Pathfinder) series.

For country walks of the type described in this book, although the Landranger maps are adequate, the Pathfinder series will be found much more helpful. The larger scale and extra detail, particularly of such things as field boundaries and antiquities, will add interest as well as assisting with route-finding. But of course they show a much smaller area than Landrangers, so you will need more of them to cover all the walks in this book.

In 1994 the Ordnance Survey published the first maps in the new Explorer series. These are also at 1:25,000 scale, but cover a much larger area than a Pathfinder. It is intended to withdraw Pathfinder sheets if they are covered by an Explorer map. As it happens, some of the walks in this book are shown on the Explorer maps of the Mendip Hills, so we have given the details for both series. But you need only have one of them.

For the benefit of those readers who have OS maps with them, and who like to follow the route or plot it on the map in advance, we have given six-figure grid references (shown as 'GR') in the text for a few key points on each walk as well as for the starting point. You will know that the first three digits show the 'east/west' position and the last three the 'north/south' position - easily remembered by the phrase 'you walk before you climb'. Please also remember that the grid reference identifies the south-west corner of a 100m square, and the point may be anywhere in that square. But if you do not find this aspect of map-reading interesting, you can ignore the grid references without hindering your enjoyment of the walk.

> *He had bought a large map representing the sea,*
> *Without the least vestige of land:*
> *And the crew were much pleased when they found it to be*
> *A map they could all understand.*
>
> *"Other maps are such shapes, with their islands and capes!*
> *But we've got our brave Captain to thank"*
> *(So the crew would protest) "that he's bought us the best -*
> *A perfect and absolute blank!"*
>> *(from* The Hunting of the Snark *by Lewis Carroll)*

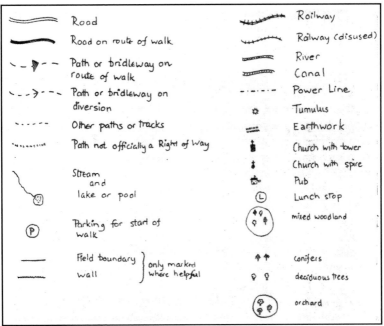

Symbols used on the walk maps

What to take with you

It is likely that you, planning to enjoy one or more of these all-day walks, are not completely new to country walking. We would not wish to discourage you from taking as much or little as you are already comfortable with. However, for those who welcome some guidance, we will describe some of the items that we might wear or carry.

Footwear is always the most important. Our own preference is for boots, ideally with some ankle support. These need not be heavy; modern lightweight fabric boots can be very comfortable and will be fully adequate except in the most adverse weather. Some prefer stout shoes. Either way, make sure the soles are well indented to give a good grip. There are those walkers who like trainers in good weather, and those who like wellingtons in bad; neither is our choice, but our advice would be merely that you should wear either of these only if you are really used to them, and happy to wear them for long distances.

Some prefer to wear two pairs of socks, but we normally do this only in mountainous country where tough, heavy boots are needed. One fairly thick pair of socks is adequate.

Wear trousers or, if you prefer, breeches. In the latter case we advise long socks as brambles and nettles can be major obstacles. For the same reason we do not recommend shorts. If, in warm weather, you wear jeans, take waterproof overtrousers unless you are certain (how can you be?) that it will not rain; jeans are notoriously slow to dry, and unpleasant while doing so.

Even if the forecast is good, on an all-day walk the weather can turn against you. Except at the height of summer, you may find it cold in the exposed country you will visit (and even a moderate wind will make it feel much colder than it is). So consider, at the least, taking a warm hat and some gloves. A windproof jacket, and the overtrousers already mentioned, are also desirable. All this leads us to suggest that you take a small rucksack (it can be one between two), as when you are out all day you will welcome the opportunity to add, or take off, a layer from time to time. And a proper sac is so much more convenient and comfortable than a carrier bag, or trying to tie things round your waist!

We would always bring a water bottle, and suggest you take some chocolate or other energy-giving food, such as nuts, to sustain you. Another suggestion is a map case. These are made of transparent plastic, are very cheap, and keep your map, or this book, dry when it rains! We do not enjoy slinging the map case round our necks (the wind always swirls it around in an attempt to throttle us), but it is quite easy to carry when needed, and stuff into the sac when the weather is dry.

Having described what we would take (and the precise list will, of course, vary with the time of year and the weather forecast), we would counsel that too much is almost as bad as too little. One of us once saw a party start out on the Cotswold Way carrying a rope! We have to hope that it was being done for a bet. You do not need to start on any of these walks as if you are about to climb Ben Nevis. No whistles, no survival bags. You do not **need** a compass, though if you like to walk with one we would not wish to discourage you. Just a good dose of common sense will be your most useful companion.

A Note on Rights of Way

[When, in the text of the book, we need to draw attention to a matter relating to a Right of Way, the relevant note will be in italics and enclosed in square brackets, as here.]

With very minor exceptions (which we have noted as they occur), all walks in this book follow Rights of Way. Although we think it unlikely that you will be challenged on any of these walks (assuming that you have not strayed from the route!), it is as well to be prepared.

It is our view that most difficulties about Rights of Way can best be resolved by a sensible and cooperative approach rather than one of confrontation. If a farmer asks us to take a slightly different route, perhaps round the edge of a field rather than across it, then we would almost always agree. Indeed, unlike some, we favour sensible diversions of Rights of Way onto routes which are more satisfactory for both walkers and landowners. Equally we can sympathise with the farmer who asked us not to describe the easier line, rather than the Right of Way; he fears ending up with two rights across his land rather than one! On the other hand, if Rights of Way are actually and deliberately blocked then it is necessary to involve the County Council. It is therefore wise to know something of the status of Rights of Way, even though you are unlikely to carry formal evidence of their existence with you! (OS maps are a good guide, but can be out of date.) We do not pretend to give a description of the legal background to such rights (which is, to say the least, complex), but hope that the following notes may help. Ultimately it is for each walker to make up his or her own mind as to the approach to adopt if a problem occurs.

Rights of Way, where they exist, **always** include the right of passage for a pedestrian. Footpath signs and waymarks will often be 'colour-coded', and then yellow indicates a path, blue a bridle-way and red a track or road open to (though not necessarily suitable for) vehicles. White is used to indicate a 'Long Distance Path' such as the Cotswold Way or the West Mendip Way; occasionally these follow 'permissive paths' which are not actually Rights of Way.

County Councils are required to maintain records of Rights of Way in their areas, and these are marked by the Ordnance Survey (in red on Landranger, and green on Pathfinder and Explorer maps). If you are following a Right of Way on foot you should not be challenged or turned off. However it is nearly always more difficult for the walker to be sure of the position than for the landowner; and a minority of the latter, regrettably, try to take advantage of this.

Temporary obstructions to Rights of Way are not uncommon, and often legal. If ploughed up, you may follow the line of the path (and the farmer should reinstate it within a fortnight of ploughing). You may also deviate from the Right of Way to avoid an obstruction provided that you do so to the minimum extent practicable.

Occasionally a Right of Way is diverted. If this has occurred in the few years before publication of this book then we draw attention to it, as OS maps will probably still show the old route, whereas we shall advise you to take the new one. If a diversion occurs after publication and you are challenged, please follow any variation that may be requested of you. Bear in mind that landowners can ask you to leave if you have no right of access. If you are told that a Right of Way has been 'extinguished' then you have some grounds for suspicion, as this is most unusual other than in extreme situations, such as the building of a new motorway. We would ask you to take up the matter with the appropriate County Council, and let us know (by writing to us, care of our publisher).

Dogs

Few topics in the walking world are more likely to arouse strong passions than that of dogs. We would not wish to enter this debate, but would say that the walks in this book have not been chosen for their suitability for your canine friend. As is common in pastoral country, there are a large number of stiles to negotiate. Not all allow dogs to get through and, depending on your dog, you may have to lift it over. You will certainly encounter sheep, and almost certainly cattle as well; these, especially if young, react adversely to dogs even on leads and there are occasional reports of injuries caused as a result. Serious problems are most unlikely but you should be aware of the risks.

If you do wish to take your dog with you, in the interests of continued cooperation with farmers and others, please make sure that you keep it on a lead at all necessary times.

Summary of the Walks

The table below shows, in summary form, information about the six walks in this book, in order to assist you in deciding which walk to choose. It records the start point (and approximately how far this is from Bath, and in which direction) and the distances and times for the walk, both before and after lunch and in total. The times are estimated as described above; they do not include the time you spend at lunch. It also shows whether there is a significant short cut described in the text. If there is, reference to the relevant chapter will tell you how much distance and time you may be able to save.

You will note that the walks starting at Stockhill Woods and Beckhampton require early starts, as it may well take you over 3 hours to reach the pub! (Unusually, the Stockhill walk has its short cut before lunch, but this will save only about a quarter of an hour.)

Walk & Starting Place (distance from Bath)	Morning		Afternoon		Total		Short Cut?
	Miles	Hours	Miles	Hours	Miles	Hours	
1. Burrington Combe (20 miles WSW)	3½	1¾	8¾	4	12¼	5¾	No
2. Stockhill Woods (18 miles SW)	7½	3½	5½	2¾	13	6¼	Yes
3. Hinton Charterhouse (5 miles S)	3¾	2	7¼	3½	11	5½	Yes
4. Box (7 miles ENE)	5	2¼	7	3¼	12	5½	Yes
5. Castle Combe (14 miles NE)	4½	2	7½	3½	12	5½	Yes
6. Beckhampton (24 miles E)	7¼	3¼	9	4	16¼	7¼	Yes

"Would you please tell me which way to go from here?" "That depends a good deal on where you want to get to" said the Cat. "I don't much care where ... " said Alice. "Then it doesn't matter which way you go."
(*from* Alice's Adventures in Wonderland *by Lewis Carroll*)

Mendip Magic

The first two walks take us to the Mendip Hills, and explore the features which go to make up this fascinating part of Somerset. It may seem wild and desolate but Man has been walking these hills for thousands of years, and has left his mark on them in many ways. Yet for all its history, it is reluctant to give up its secrets. Even the manner of the formation of some of its geological features remains a puzzle. Nor is it certain whether the high plateau has always been treeless, or whether Man is responsible. His presence among these hills has been traced back nearly half a million years, although the oldest features that we shall explore date back a mere 4 to 5,000 years, to Neolithic and Iron Age times.

Mendip is a rich area for naturalists, with many rare plants and animals. Once a Royal Hunting Forest, with strict penalties against poaching, the old name, Mendip Forest, has been revived by the Forestry Commission. Not all the planting is of softwoods; there are mixed plantations, and the Commission is interested in the recreational and environmental uses of the forest as well as the commercial.

The area is now best known for its caves, and particularly at weekends you may meet groups of people kitted out in overalls, helmets and torches, ready to explore the depths, or see them returning, muddy and tired. Yet for most of its history Mendip was an industrialised area. From very early times, Man has been at work, extracting the many minerals found in the area. The most common are lead ores, but some are extremely rare: one is even called Mendipite, for it is found nowhere else. Traces of these activities are still visible, as we shall see during the walks. Excavations at the Glastonbury Lake Villages have revealed lead, and its use can certainly be dated back to the first millenium BC. In Roman times, British lead was so abundant that Spain, also an exporter, complained, and a limit was put on production. The Great Bath at Bath (Aquae Sulis) is lined with Mendip lead, and pigs (lead ingots) supplied by the 2nd legion have been discovered in France. Most such pigs are identifiable by the words "BRIT EX ARG VEB", i.e. British lead from the silver works at Veb. We can identify Charterhouse as the silver works, and Veb. is a shortened form of the Roman name for the area. Unfortunately we do not know the full name, but some have speculated that it survives in the name Ubley, a village overlooking Blagdon Lake.

In the Middle Ages, hilltop Mendip was divided into four mineries known as 'Liberties' - Priddy, Harptree, Chewton and Charterhouse -

under the command of the four Lords Royal of Mendip: the Bishop of Bath and Wells, and the Lords of Harptree, Chewton, and Charterhouse. It was a bishop who codified the ten rules which governed the miners, including the harsh burning out with which a thief was punished. He was confined with his tools in his house or hut which was then set on fire. If he was fortunate he escaped, never to return to Mendip.

The industry's peak was in the 17th century, but from then on it went into decline, until some Cornish entrepreneurs in the early 19th century decided they could resmelt the old heaps. For a time this was fairly effective, but by 1880 nearly all the mineries had closed. It is this industry which has left the most enduring relics, which we pass on the two walks.

In eastern Mendip, coal has been found, and, by contrast with these 'dirty' industries, paper-making also flourished, using the clear streams. Quarrying has made a more dramatic impact, the large-scale operations of recent times being particularly controversial.

Yet despite its industrial past, and the demands of modern times, Mendip remains an area of peace and tranquillity.

Vespasian, legate of the 2nd legion Augusta in south-west Britain, 43-47AD

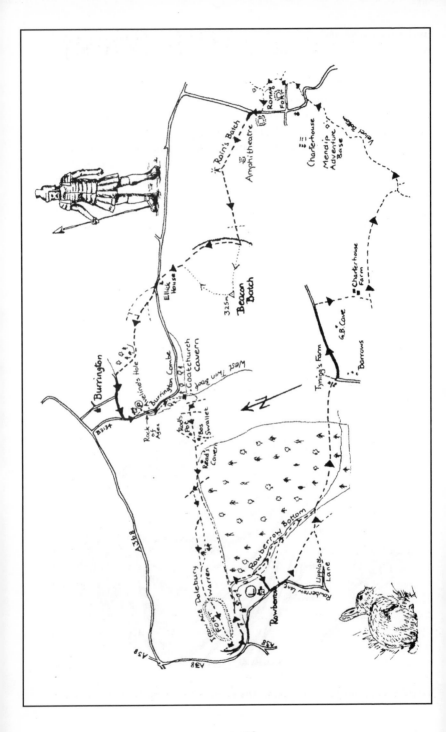

Burrington

B3134

Rock of Ages

Aveline's Hole

Burrington Combe

Goatchurch Cavern

West Twin Brook

Rod's Pot

Bos Swallet

Read's Cavern

Elk's Hole

Ellick House

325m △

Beacon Batch

Rain's Batch

Amphitheatre

Rains FORT

Charterhouse

Mendip Adventure Base

Charterhouse Farm

G.B. Cave

Barrows

Tyning's Farm

Rowberrow Bottom

Dolebury Warren

IRON AGE FORT

Rowberrow Lane

Lippiatt Lane

A368

A38

A38

18

1   Mendip Hills (West)

Location   The north-western part of the Mendip Hills,
about 32 km (20 miles) west-south-west of Bath

Distance   5½ km (3½ miles) before lunch
13¾ km (8¾ miles) after lunch

Time   1¾ hours before lunch
4 hours after lunch

Maps   Landranger 182 (Weston-super-Mare & Bridgwater)
(nearly all the walk is on Landranger 172 also)
Explorer 4 (Mendip Hills West)
or (former) Pathfinder 1198 (Cheddar)

Start   The 'Rock of Ages' car park at the foot of Burrington Combe, on the B3134 (GR 476588)

Lunch   *The Swan* at Rowberrow (GR 450582)
Tel: 01934 852371

The starting point for this walk is at the bottom (north end) of Burrington Combe, a fine gorge to the north of the better-known one at Cheddar. You are likely to approach by using the A368 road, which runs between Weston-super-Mare and Bath. About 2½ km (1½ miles) west of Blagdon, or 3 km (2 miles) east of Churchill, turn south on the B3134 (signposted Burrington Combe). The car park is about 750m (½ mile) from this junction on your left, shortly after a garden centre and a pub/restaurant (the Burrington Inn). Make sure that you lock your car and hide any valuables, as this tends to be a popular spot for thieves.

This walk begins with an immediate opportunity to see the geology of Mendip. The two principal layers are the Old Red Sandstone (about 400 million years old) and Carboniferous Limestone, sandwiched between some very ancient rocks and a thin layer at the top from the Triassic and Jurassic periods. While the limestone was still young, some major folding occurred, and evidence of it can clearly be seen in the cliffs behind the car park where you will leave the car. Combes and gorges such as the one at Burrington, and more famously that at Cheddar, were once thought to have been caused by cave collapses; now it is believed that they are due to water erosion, but it is still not certain, since most water tends to permeate through the limestone, forming the caves and pot-holes for which this area is famous. Across the road from the car park is a cleft in the rock where in 1775 the Rev Augustus Montague Toplady took shelter from a storm. This inspired him to compose one of the most popular hymns ever written, *Rock of Ages*.

During the first section of the walk you should be looking out for caves, for there is a fine selection in this area. (**Under no circumstances should you consider entering them; even experienced cavers can come to grief**.) On your left as you walk up the combe you will see **Aveline's Hole**, close to the roadside. This was discovered in 1797 when the pile of stones in front of the entrance was, by chance, removed. Human bones were found, as well as shells, birds and mammals, the widest variety ever discovered. There are also some popular swallets in this stretch (formed when a stream is swallowed up into the limestone), notably Sidcot. Another local name for this phenomenon is 'slocker'. This happens to the brook that you meet early in the walk, West Twin Brook. After heavy rain it sometimes runs on to another swallet, so you may meet it earlier than we indicate, and have to cross it twice, to the right and then to the left.

Cross the road and turn L, to follow a clear (if narrow) path into the gorge below the rocks. The Rock of Ages faces you as you cross the road, and Aveline's Hole is just a few metres up on the left-hand side. For 350m this path runs alongside the road; then (at a small lay-by which is marked "No Parking Please - Cave Rescue Only") it veers slightly R and starts climbing. You are in a heavily wooded gorge with a little stream, the West Twin Brook, running down it. When you reach the stream, cross it (to the left) and climb for 20m or so up a rather steep bank or, if the stream is fairly dry, you can follow up the stream itself. The path then levels off and shortly returns to the stream, which you cross again (to the right) by a trough.

Just before crossing at the trough, you will notice a rocky path going up to the left. It leads to the two entrances to another well-known cave, **Goatchurch Cavern**, known as the Main Entrance and Back Door (or Tradesman's Entrance). This cave has some interesting formations such as The Dining Room, and the Giant's Stairs, which take you to the lower level. An attempt was made in 1900 to open it as a show cave, but happily for the tranquillity of Burrington Combe, it came to nothing.

Continue up the path (with the stream now on your left) for another 250m or so. (In these woods there are a number of variant paths. It is not critical exactly which route you take, so long as you stay fairly close to the stream rather than go more steeply uphill, away from it, and so long as you finish with it on your left.) During this stretch you should emerge from the woodland into open, bracken-covered hillside. After this 250m you will come to a path crossing yours.

At this junction the path you are on continues up the valley of the stream and a rather wider path comes across that valley. It is currently, and discreetly waymarked "Limestone Link", though such signs have a habit of disappearing from time to time. You should turn sharp R and follow the Limestone Link, gently uphill at first. You will bear round to the L at one point, and you will cross some more junctions, but make sure that you take the path ahead at each of them. As the track levels out you will see more established woods ahead, both to left and right, and your track makes for a fairly obvious corner about 700m (nearly half a mile) from the junction already mentioned (where you met the Limestone Link).

Very close to this corner are two typical Mendip potholes, **Rod's Pot** to the right and **Bos Swallet** on the left. You can see the entrances at the foot of two dips, looking rather like old bomb craters, but **you are warned not to get too close**, as these, like other potholes, can be very dangerous for the inexperienced. They are more difficult to enter than caves. Rod's Pot is described as having an entrance squeeze - to non-cavers it looks impenetrable. Bos Swallet was found to contain items such as ox bones, flints, and beaker pottery, but it is now thought that these were dumped there by miners who, in the course of their activities, destroyed the remains of some Iron Age settlement from which they came. A draught blows out from the swallet in summer, but blows inwards in winter. More interesting historically is the nearby **Read's Cavern**, which is further along, hidden in a hollow away to your left. This was occupied during the Iron Age, and contained some interesting items, including some horse hobbles. The occupants were trapped when it suffered a collapse. The main chamber is 150 feet long, though there are other chambers as well.

*After passing the potholes your route continues straight ahead, and soon meets an old stone wall which you keep on your right . (Read's Cavern is tucked away in a dip a little way along on the left-hand side.) You are not far from the conifer plantation (which is Rowberrow Warren) on your left but you should never quite reach it. Instead, 600m after the potholes you come to another, very clear track crossing yours. Here you turn R, and after only 75m turn L over a stile into **Dolebury** (pronounced Dollbury) **Warren Nature Reserve**. There is a National Trust sign at this point, as well as one describing the reserve.*

You have just entered the nature reserve which will eventually lead you out on to **Dolebury Warren**, the most spectacular feature on this walk, particularly on a clear day. It is one of the many Iron Age hill forts in this area, which vary so greatly that it is possible that the term 'fort' is misleading. They may be anything from a simple farm to a town, although they seem to have a defensive aspect. Rather unusually, the fort does not enclose the summit of the hill, which is at one corner. As a result, to the south and west, Dolebury is almost impregnable, though the inhabitants might have had a problem finding drinking water. Since it was first constructed in the Middle Iron Age, it has had many uses. In the fifth century, as Roman rule disintegrated, it is possible that it again became a centre of population, but by the Middle Ages, it was being used to farm rabbits. Long banks called pillow mounds can still be seen, and most authorities agree these date from the Middle Ages and were constructed to encourage the rabbits to burrow. However one local gentleman of the late 19th century insisted they were vermin traps and said he remembered when they were not there. It seems possible that his memory misled him, for records of these warrens with their mounds date back to the 13th century. In 1665 there was a petition to the king asking him to prevent Jonathan Duckman from building new warrens, for the rabbits damaged the grass on which the villagers' cattle grazed. The ruins of a cottage through which the path passes are all that is left of the warrener's home. There was still a warrener about 100 years ago. Ochre has been mined here, and stories of finding 'fairy pipes' are prosaically explained; they are the miners' clay tobacco pipes. There is a romantic tradition that minerals more valuable than iron lie buried here. Leland quoted:

If Dolbyri digged were,
Of gold shulde be the share.

It also has a surprising collection of plants. Geologically the hill is limestone, so on the summit and to the south will be found the lime-loving plants, but windborne sand means that an acidic soil can be found on the northwest side, giving a home to plants that could not live on other parts of the hill. As they drop leaf litter, so the acidity increases.

Proceed straight ahead along the obvious path, initially with woodland on your left, to a fence corner. Cross the stile to your right, veering R from your original line, and following a path which leads between trees and bushes to and along the crest of the hill. There seem to be a number of paths ahead, but you should stay close to the crest of the ridge, keeping a small plantation on your left, until you reach the highest point. The summit is 3¹/₄ km (2 miles) and just over 1 hour from the start (at GR 453590), and is an excellent viewpoint where you may well wish to linger. You may therefore find it helpful to know that the lunch point is only about 45 minutes from here.

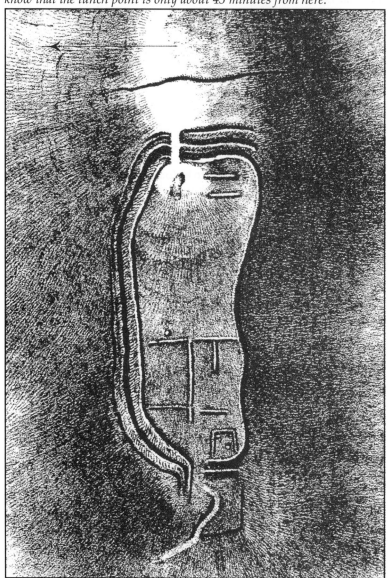

Dolebury hill fort from A History of Somerset *by Rev W. Phelps (1834)*

When you finally reach the summit you will have perhaps the best views on Mendip: to the east is **Blagdon Lake**; northwards are the cooling towers at **Portishead**; west (the direction in which you have been walking) is the **Bristol Channel**, with the islands of **Steep Holm** and **Flat Holm** clearly visible and the Welsh hills beyond; south-west are **Wavering Down** and **Crook Peak** (a tautological name for those who collect them: Cruc is a Celtic word for peak) and beyond them the **Somerset Levels** with the hills of south Somerset hazily visible even further away; to the south you are looking in the direction of **Cheddar** (which is, of course, hidden by the main Mendip ridge). The two islands acquired their Scandinavian name of Holm during the 9th century when they were occupied by Vikings. Flat Holm is part of Wales but Steep Holm is the most westerly extent of Mendip, and was once the home of some Augustinian priors. In later centuries it has been a haven for smugglers, a garrison, and now a nature reserve, administered by a trust. Among the unusual plants to be found there are the wild paeony (*paeonia mascula*), perhaps taken there by the monks.

When you decide to proceed, continue ahead (west) but bearing slightly L from the direction you took on the approach, making for a very clear path further down the grassy slopes leading to a clear notch in the far ramparts. Join this and, once through the notch, follow it into the woods; here the path turns L and almost immediately curves round to the R, and you follow it, ignoring turnings on the left. Go downhill in the woods, and through the exit gate from the Reserve (ignore the track bearing right when the gate is in sight); continue for 50m to a very narrow driveway in the village of Dolebury Bottom, where you turn sharp L. Continue to a lane which gradually curves further left until it degenerates into a muddy track, and you pass through a gate (with an entry back into the Reserve on the left, leading to a steep uphill path, which you ignore). Continue ahead for some 700m (nearly ½ mile) after this gate, when you should see, on the right, a rather narrow field and just beyond it a signed footpath - yet again, part of the Limestone Link. Turn R to take this path.

You are now entering **Rowberrow Bottom**, a peaceful valley now, but where once there was a rather mean, industrial village. Until about 150 years ago, **Rowberrow**, with its neighbouring village of **Shipham**, was the centre of the calamine mining industry, and had been so since the 16th century. One account of Shipham, written in 1792, speaks of more than 100 mines "in the streets, in the yards, and in the very houses". Calamine is a zinc ore and was needed for brass-making. In 1738, William Champion of Bristol discovered the process to extract zinc from the ore; his brass works at Warmley became the largest producer in Europe, and the needs of that factory made this area a hive of industry. Nearly every villager was involved in the work and it was said that when worked ceased, "they may be seen crawling out of the mines exactly like rabbits from their burrows". The women and children probably picked over and sorted the ore; certainly women and children were seen at such a task near Priddy, in 1820.

There are still signs of its past: Shipham has what is believed to be a calamine oven, and at Rowberrow Church, there is the grave of a man "crushed to death in a mine". The boom was over by 1853, and the miners at Rowberrow and Shipham had to walk to **Charterhouse** every day to work at the mines there, where refuse from the old lead mines was being reprocessed. Their route become known as 'The Slaggers' Path'; you will be walking a small part of it in the afternoon. As you walk through the valley you will see the ruins of the former cottages.

You will soon come to a gate leading into the garden of a house. In fact, there is a Right of Way through this gate, and if you have brought a picnic and do not need to visit the pub, you may prefer to take it, following the alternative route described below. If, however, you do want lunch at the pub, you do not go straight on; instead, bear R on an enclosed track which leads uphill for 80m to a lane which is a public road. Turn R again on reaching this, and walk for 250m through the small village of Rowberrow to a road T-junction. Here you will see The Swan on your right, and this is the suggested lunch spot (5½ km, 3½ miles, and 1¾ hours from the start; GR 450582).

Alternative route through Rowberrow Bottom: continue along the valley, keeping the stream on your left. (Do not miss the well-preserved limekiln on the left.) After about 800m the path and stream swing round to the left, and you will pass a small structure belonging to Bristol Waterworks. A path comes in steeply from the right, and you will see a West Mendip Way waymark. At this point you have rejoined the full route at the beginning of the second paragraph of instructions after the lunch stop.

If you feel you have arrived rather early for lunch, you might like to visit the church, which is about 400m beyond the pub, downhill. It is kept locked, but the grave of the crushed miner is by the porch door, its stone now greatly eroded. In summer, roses overhang the grave, as they do many parts of the churchyard. Return to the pub for lunch.

This pub has been an inn for over 200 years, and in Rowberrow's heyday must have been rather riotous. The two villages, Rowberrow and Shipham, were notorious for the roughness of their inhabitants.

Hannah More and her sister, who were trying to set up Sunday Schools in an effort to bring some civilisation to Mendip, described them as follows: "Among the most depraved and wretched were Shipham and Rowberrow, two mining villages at the top of Mendip: the people savage and depraved almost even beyond Cheddar, brutal in their natures, and ferocious in their manners. ... No constable would venture to arrest a Shipham man, lest he should be concealed in one of their pits, and never heard of more; no uncommon case." This pub must have been the scene of some interesting encounters in those violent days. Today, it is a pleasant hostelry, with the landlord's collection of engines and tools adorning the walls and shelves. There are also some old pictures of Rowberrow showing the houses in Rowberrow Bottom.

And Noah he cocked his eye and said, "It looks like rain, I think;
The water has drowned the Matterhorn as deep as a Mendip mine,
But I don't care where the water goes if it doesn't get into the wine".
(from Wine and Water, *by G.K.Chesterton)*

After lunch, on emerging from the front door of The Swan you want to turn L and follow the road, gently uphill, for 250m. (Note: do not turn L twice to return down School Lane, the lane by which you arrived.) After this distance the road (called Rowberrow Lane) bears right (and there is a private drive ahead) but you want to veer L along a track. This is called Holloway Lane, though its name is not shown anywhere; it proceeds upwards for about 700m (nearly ½ mile) until it reaches a small group of houses. Here there is another 'crossroads' of paths or tracks. You want to take the left-hand one (though you are only bearing L, not really turning) which goes downhill in a ditch very much enclosed by vegetation. This track used to be very muddy but recent work has improved its surface greatly. At this junction you join the West Mendip Way. This (which we shall abbreviate WMW) is a very fine Long Distance Path running from the sea just south of Weston-super-Mare for 45km (28 miles) to Wells Cathedral: on your walk today you will follow it for some 5 km (3 miles). The WMW has some very distinctive waymarks and while you follow it they will be directing you to Cheddar. This is rather odd as the Way does not actually go to the village of Cheddar, but that is not our problem!

You are briefly using part of the slaggers' route to Charterhouse; you are walking it for pleasure, but they had to set out early every morning, and then trail home again in the evening after a long and arduous day at the lead works. The lane which came in from the right at the junction is thought by some to be a Roman road, leading from the coast at Uphill to Charterhouse. This is not certain; it may even be a pre-Roman track. It is called **Lippiatt Lane**, a name occuring in other parts of Mendip. It is thought to come from the Saxon word *lepegeate* referring to a barrier between the farm lands and the Royal Forest. There is also Deerleap at Wookey, and another 'gate' name, Rhodyates, occurs at two locations. The Royal Forest was for hunting and there were severe penalties for poaching. These were often ignored. In the 13th century, not only were the Rector and Clerk of Shipham found guilty of poaching, but certain Carthusian monks were discovered running a deer-trapping scheme.

*The track in the ditch lasts only 250m when you emerge into a narrow valley containing a small stream. You want to bear R (upstream). It does not matter whether you cross the stream here and turn R (keeping the little fenced plantation on your right), or whether you follow the current WMW waymarks (they have changed, and could change again) to the right of the plantation, and cross the stream 200m further on. But, one way or the other, you must cross the stream. (There is no helpful footbridge, but even on one flooded February day we had no difficulty jumping across!) After the upper stream crossing there is a clear track bearing L away from the stream and gently upwards into the woodland (another part of Rowberrow Warren), which you must take. This is still part of the WMW. The slaggers turned slightly left here to take them directly over the top of **Blackdown**, but we are going to Charterhouse by the pretty route.*

From time to time you may see some iron posts marked ARDC, a relic of the old Axbridge Rural District Council, and dating from the early 1900s. We found two flung in the stream. The woodland around you is managed by Forest Enterprise, and is used for purely forestry purposes of timber production. Strictly speaking they do not supply recreational facilities here as they do at other sites, but many Rights of Way criss-cross it.

Keep going along the woodland track. After nearly 1 km (over ½ mile) you meet another track crossing yours in the form of an inverted 'U', but you go straight across and very soon afterwards come to a gate leading out of the woods. The track continues in open country for 450m to Tyning's Farm (2¾ km, 1¾ miles and 45 minutes from The Swan; GR 470565). You want to continue on from Tyning's Farm in the same direction as your approach. To do this, as you reach the farm you bear slightly L to pass through with just one set of buildings on your left. Then immediately turn R for just 40m, and then L when you meet the road at a corner. You will be following this road for very nearly 1 km (rather over ½ mile), though it seems rather longer than this.

The name **Tyning's Farm** refers to the enclosed fields on which a tithe would have been payable. It is one of the oldest farms on Mendip, and is a junction of roads, paths and bridleways some of which are no longer as important as they once were. A bridleway that you will see veering off to your left as you reach the road was once the Bristol road to Cheddar. Before walking along, look over the gate into the field on your right. There are three barrows here with two more close by, which have all been excavated. Three are burial mounds, each constructed differently from the others. There are several caves and swallets in the area. Most notably, a little further along, and hidden from view by the uneven ground is a very popular cave with the pedestrian name of GB Cave. It has the largest main chamber known in the Mendip area, with 1^1/$_4$ miles of explored passages.

*After walking along the road, turn R down a farm access lane signed to Charterhouse and Piney Sleight Farms, and still part of the WMW. Pass Charterhouse Farm by keeping a thick windbreak of conifers immediately to your right, veering R up a slight rise. You soon reach a junction of paths where you turn L, following the WMW and keeping a wall on your right hand. Follow this line, tending slightly to the R and passing a number of stiles; after nearly 1 km (^{1}/$_2$ mile) you enter some woods and the path goes more noticeably downhill. 300m after entering the woods, you reach a valley bottom and for the next few minutes **you need to take particular care with your route-finding**, especially as the WMW is not very clearly waymarked in this area.*

On reaching the valley, go over the stile ahead and walk on in the same direction, in a delightful grassy hollow, for 175m. At this point (GR 487549) the valley turns to the right, and there is a wall on your left. In this wall there is firstly a stone stile, and secondly a gate. You should cross the stile, bearing L into a side valley which goes very gradually upwards. (Do not turn more sharply L to follow a faint path going up the hillside.) It is at this point, incidentally, that you leave the WMW, which goes on down the main valley to the right. If you have successfully followed these manoeuvres, you are now in Velvet Bottom and your navigational problems are at an end.

Velvet Bottom is a fascinating and attractive piece of industrial archaeology, heading roughly east though with a number of 'wiggles'. You will pass, and have to climb, several low dams - but you need not worry, the time is long past when they held any water. Their construction is thought to be connected with lead-mining, which we will investigate when we come to Charterhouse. On the way there, notice how short the grass is: this is due to the many rabbits that live in this area. You can see why the 17th-century local smallholders were so unenthusiastic about warrens. Here and there you may find neat squares cut out of the turf, where keen gardeners have decided to use the soft green carpet to repair their lawns. This area, now a Nature Reserve, is rich in wild-life, and on a hot summer's day you may see a wide variety of butterflies such as the Marbled White (*Melanargia galathea*). You may also find the occasional adder. These snakes also like to bask in this sheltered valley, but they are far more nervous of you than you of them, so they will probably take cover as they hear your approach. The great heaps of black glassy slag through which you are passing are the remnants of 19th-century resmelting of old waste heaps, into which many rabbits seem to have burrowed. One would think it made for a rather uncomfortable home.

Follow the track along this valley; if the track splits then it does not matter which branch you take as they will join up again, but do not climb out of the valley on either side. About 1¼ km (¾ mile) after entering Velvet Bottom you will pass a smallish, unattractive hut on your left. This is the Mendip Adventure Base, and it is some 7 km (4½ miles) and 2 hours from your lunch point. In a further 450m you reach a minor road. (In 1968, flash-flooding after torrential rain caused this section of road to be swept away, hence the vast drainage pipe beneath the road.) *Go ahead along this road for 75m and then, before it curves right over a bank, bear L through a gate.*

You are in the midst of the lead industry at Charterhouse. Below you those strange circular depressions are 'buddles', the Cornish method which the 19th-century resmelters used to extract lead ore from the refuse. The floor of the buddle was slightly convex, and when a stream of water was fed into the middle of it by what is called a 'launder', and circulated by hanging brushes, the heavier ore stayed in the middle while the lighter dirt was washed away. This heavy mud, known graphically as 'slimes', was then resmelted. Those dams you saw earlier may have been an attempt to catch any ore that was washed away when the buddles were emptied. High on the hillside to your right, as well as in the valley itself, the ground is extremely uneven, and is known as gruffy ground, because the trenches the miners dug were called gruffs or grooves. There are also shafts in the area, so stay on the track!

Walk along the clear track which curves round to the left for 250m to the end of another minor road. On your right is a small car park (at GR 505557). (Here you will find some boards with an explanation of the area which is now a Field Study and Outdoor Activity Centre. As you may guess by its name, Charterhouse originally belonged to Carthusian monks, based at Witham. Of this original Friary almost nothing remains, but their presence on Mendip has survived in the name of this village, where the monks had a farmstead.) *Go through the car park and bear round to the L, negotiating a gate and following a track signed to "Nordrach". Ignore paths branching off to the right; instead keep going gently round to the L until, 250m after leaving the car park, you will find a path turning L and slightly downhill, keeping a large mound on its left. Take this path.*

You are now crossing a dam which created the reservoir of water to supply the buddles, though it is now silted up. As you walk across, you may notice to your left a large enclosure, the remnant of the Roman fort which held the mine-workers: slaves and prisoners of war. It was also a control point for the lead.

Roman pig (ingot) of Mendip lead

Cross the dam, a stream and a stile and walk up the left-hand edge of a field to a road. Turn R and follow this road for 160m, taking care, for it can be quite busy for such a minor road, to a junction where you turn L and go noticeably uphill past a farm. You are now on a minor cul-de-sac known as Rains Batch, away from the traffic.

Stop after a little while and look back across the valley to see the clear evidence of mining in the area you have just come through. Directly across the valley you should now be able to see the condenser flues on the hillside. The smelting furnace was directly below it. A forced draught caused vaporisation, the gases then passing up the flues. The soot was then scraped off and resmelted. Three-quarters of all recovered lead came from this soot. Silver was found here; the Romans referred to this as the silver works, and during the 19th century it was extracted using the Pattinson process.

The first field on your left is called Town Field, referring to the Roman settlement in this area. In fact, most of the settlement lay to your right, but there have been several finds in this field. Sheep and cows are said to have died by feeding off its grass, which was heavily impregnated with lead. There is a medieval enclosure in this field, but two fields further up Rains Batch, also on your left, is a circular enclosure about which archaeologists are not certain but which could be a Roman amphitheatre.

At the top of Rains Batch, some 750m from the road, you reach a wireless station with several prominent masts which you will no doubt have noticed earlier on during the walk. Unless you make the diversion to Beacon Batch in a few minutes time, this is the highest point, at 311m (1,020 feet) on this walk or indeed, by a tiny margin, any of the walks in this book. The wireless station is 9½ km (6 miles) and 2¾ hours from Rowberrow, at GR 498568.

You have emerged on to the open plateau of Blackdown, which still retains the wild nature of much of Mendip before the enclosures of the 18th and 19th centuries. Typically for Mendip summits, it is sandstone rather than limestone, and the bilberry (*vaccinium myrtillus*), known locally as the wortleberry, grows here quite abundantly. When local people come to gather the fruit, they describe this activity as 'wortling'.

On reaching the wireless station, bear L along a clear track, leaving the masts to your right, and go gently downhill. After ¾ km (½ mile), at about the lowest point, a signed footpath crosses your track; ignore this, and go on for another 150m to an old wall. Cross this indistinct wall and ditch at a gap and turn immediately R to take a path which stays close to the wall and soon starts to descend. After 800 m (½ mile) you meet other paths coming in from your left; you go straight on down the track and soon pass outbuildings and a house with iron gates to emerge on a road (the B3134).

> *If you want to climb Beacon Batch then, instead of turning R after crossing the old wall, veer only slightly R and take another clear path. Make sure you head towards the highest point on the horizon. The summit of Beacon Batch is only about 600m away. At an altitude of 325m or 1,066 feet this is the highest point of the Mendip Hills and as such, a worthwhile objective in itself; but it has to be said that the nearby terrain is rather dull and, because the summit is only slightly convex, the views not as good as you have had earlier on this walk.*
>
> *The top is adorned with an OS trig point on a grassy mound so you will be in no doubt when you have reached it. To rejoin the main walk, turn R through exactly 90° at the trig point and follow a clear path (veering R at a junction) to a tree-lined corner, where you bear L to join the track already described about 300m before it reaches the road.*

31

On reaching the road bear L and follow it for 120m to the next bend. Cross over to the car park on the opposite side and take the wide, clear stony track that leaves the left-hand side of this car park. After 100m or so there is a path off to your left which you must ignore (it does lead back to your starting point, but it finishes with a dangerously steep descent); but apart from that one, you want to take care for a while always to bear L and not to take any paths going right. Only 25m after that path to the left, you reach a Y-junction on the brow of the hill. Bear L. You should soon find yourself descending a hillside and tending in a leftwards direction rather than going straight down. After something like 800m from the road you will be in a hollow containing low scrub, and soon your path bears round to the R and continues downhill. (Do not take any paths that go upwards. You now take the right-hand path at junctions.) You continue downwards, the path becoming clearer as you descend, and about 400m from the hollow you emerge on a lane (it is in fact a private road, but a Public Bridleway) and will see a few houses below. Turn L.

(It has to be said that the route described above is not the easiest to follow, especially as the area of woodland is by no means as clearly defined as the OS maps would have you believe. But so long as you, having left the car park and breasted the slight rise for the first 200m, descend towards the large valley in front (i.e. to the north), preferably keeping L rather than R, you will come to no harm; there are several paths but all emerge lower down on a lane or track. If, when you reach this, you turn L you will soon rejoin the 'correct' route.)

You are now only ³⁄₄ km (¹⁄₂ mile) from the end of the walk, and entering the village of Burrington, rarely visited, unlike the neighbouring combe. Follow the lane downhill to a junction of minor roads. Take the left-hand one (almost straight on, in fact; not uphill, which is a private drive) unless you wish to make a detour to visit the church, in which case you should take the turning on the right. This church, which is usually open, is well worth seeing.

Burrington Church, dating from the 15th century, has an attractive porch and some very amusing gargoyles. One is the carving of a grinning man with a water-pot on his shoulder, which must look effective when fulfilling its purpose of being a drainpipe. In the churchyard are two venerable yew trees, both possibly over 500 years old, and a 15th-century preaching cross. Inside, there is a window containing old glass, and in the chancel wall you can see a stone panel. Thought to be a medieval Easter sepulchre, it shows Christ flanked by two angels, with two kneeling figures, and is unusual for the fluidity of the carving. The rambling one-time vicarage is partly Georgian and there is a happy mixture of modern houses and older cottages built of the local stone.

If you have made this detour, return to the other lane (now turning R at the junction), which brings you in a few minutes to the main B3134. Here you turn L again, past a garden centre and then a pub and restaurant, the Burrington Inn, which is usually open all day, so you may wish to stop for a well-earned snack. The car park (where there are some public conveniences) is on your left, only 100m further on, a total of 13¾ km (8¾ miles) and 4 hours from The Swan at Rowberrow.

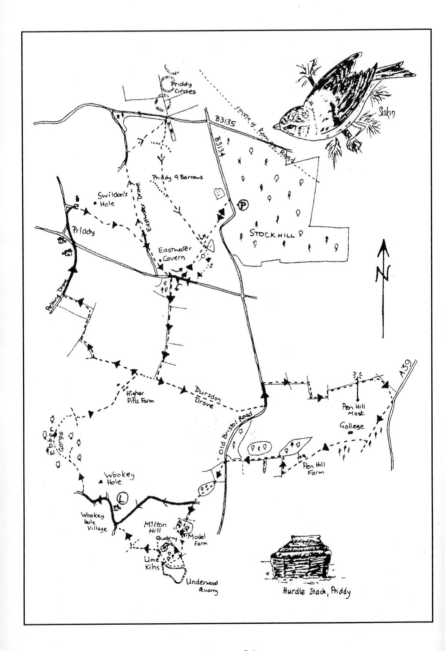

Priddy Circles

B3135

Course of Roman Road

Siskin

B3134

Priddy 9 Barrows

Swildon's Hole

Eastwater Drove

P

STOCKHILL

Priddy

Eastwater Cavern

Rolling Brook

Durston Drove

A39

Higher Pitts Farm

Ebbor Gorge

Old Bristol Road

Pen Hill Mast

College

Pen Hill Farm

Wookey Hole

Wookey Hole Village

Milton Hill

Quarry

Model Farm

Lime Kilns

Underwood Quarry

Hurdle Stack, Priddy

34

2   Mendip Hills (East)

Location	About 29 km (18 miles) south-west of Bath, and just north of Wells
Distance	12 km (7½ miles) before lunch 8¾ km (5½ miles) after lunch
Time	3½ hours before lunch 2¾ hours after lunch
Maps	Landranger 182 (Weston-super-Mare & Bridgwater) or 183 (Yeovil & Frome) Explorer 4 (Mendip Hills West) or (former) Pathfinders 1198 (Cheddar) and 1218 (Wells)
Start	Stockhill Woods car park (GR 549512)
Lunch	*Wookey Hole Inn*, Wookey Hole (GR 532475) Tel: 01749 672236 (accommodation available)

The starting point for this walk is the car park and picnic area on the west side of Stockhill Woods, which is best approached from the north via West Harptree and the B3134. On entering the car park (under a large iron bar which is intended to prevent high vehicles from using it) there is a fairly short, circular drive through the trees which you should follow round to the left (clockwise). There are many parking bays off this drive. When you leave you should continue round the drive in the same direction, as it is 'one-way traffic'. You will soon return to the entry/exit point.

You may wonder why we have called this walk 'Mendip Hills (East)' when you are still on the map named Mendip Hills West. Strictly speaking, the Mendips start at the coast near Weston-super-Mare and go east and slightly south as far as Frome. However for practical purposes the main part of the range runs north-west / south-east, from Crook Peak near the M5 to Pen Hill near Wells. This walk covers the eastern part of that main range. If you have also done our Mendip Hills (West) walk you will find it interesting to note how different the two regions are.

Notice that this walk may take you well over 3 hours before lunch, so you will need an early start. (There is a short cut as you approach the pub, but this will not save more than a quarter of an hour or so.) You may wonder why, as this walk is longer in the morning than in the afternoon, we did not suggest that it is walked in the opposite direction. This is partly because we feel that the views are more attractive this way round. It is also because, if reversed, you would have to descend Ebbor Gorge, which we would not advise unless you are an experienced walker in mountain country.

This woodland area is managed by Forest Enterprise and leased from the Waldegrave family. Once, the Romans had lead and zinc works here, a Roman road passing through the north-east corner of the woods. By the 1940s there was simply bare moorland, pitted with the remains of lead workings, at which time a decision was taken to plant 500 acres of this moorland with mixed woodland. Although the trees are mainly coniferous and 'harvested' as timber, here at Stockhill, Forest Enterprise is also concerned with recreation and conservation. Together with the Fieldfare Trust, they have marked out an Easy Going Trail, which allows wheelchair users and others with disabilities the chance to enjoy woodlands, and to observe nature at close hand. The woods are a safe home for roe deer, not to mention many varieties of birds, including siskin and sparrowhawks. If you see a large, rather scruffy-looking bird of prey circling over the forest, you are watching a buzzard. Other wildlife may well be observed during the walk: there are several areas in the hills which are nature reserves, but even in the open fields before you reach the Pen Hill mast, hares can sometimes be seen.

Return to the point at which you entered the car park from the road, cross the road, turn R and walk along the road for 100m or so when there is a clear path on the L by an indicator board. Take this path, which is mostly well-surfaced and fairly flat despite the undulating terrain, and follow it for 1¼ km (¾ mile).

This uneven ground marks the site of St Cuthbert's Leadworks. Within the Priddy Minery, these leadworks were built about 1850 when Nicholas Ennor, a Cornishman, saw the opportunity to produce lead from old waste tips. At first all went well, but he was soon involved in a lawsuit with a leadworks in the neighbouring Chewton Minery, whose owners, in an effort to throw him out of business, captured all the water needed to supply the buddles. (For an explanation of buddles you should see page 29.) He sent his workmen out to restore the water and the courts supported his right to the water in 1860. However, just a year later Ennor found himself again embroiled in a lawsuit, this time as the defendant. Again the trouble was water. The works were shown to be polluting the water used by Hodgkinsons' Paper Mill at Wookey. This was affecting the manufacture of paper, hence the lawsuit. The Hodgkinsons won after a two-year legal battle, with the court ruling that all water had to be pollution-free. This excluded the use of buddles, making the leadworks almost inoperable. Ennor sold out to a fellow Cornishman who rejoiced in the name of Horatio Nelson Hornblower. He began by pumping and re-using the water, but later installed furnaces to resmelt the slag directly. This, however, was not as efficient as the old method. Nevertheless, after various vicissitudes, St Cuthbert's was the last operative leadworks on Mendip, finally closing in 1908. Time is slowly obliterating these industrial traces, but more remain here than at Charterhouse, and of course the pools, reservoirs for the minery, are now well-established features. You will pass a restored minery building which is now used as a base for cavers and very handy for the nearby St Cuthbert's Swallet.

You pass the cavers' base on your left, and soon thereafter emerge on a minor road. Turn R and walk along the road for 300m, and turn L over a stile to take a signed footpath. Initially this path follows a wood on your right. Follow the field boundary straight ahead, always keeping to the left of the wall, and crossing several field boundaries, until (about 1¼ km or ¾ mile from the road) you come to a clear track (Dursdon Drove). Turn L and follow this track for 1½ km (nearly 1 mile); it is almost straight, apart from a left-hand bend near the end. At this point you reach another road, which is the old road between Bristol and Wells (4½ km, 2¾ miles and 1¼ hours from the start; GR 552488).

On reaching this road, turn L and walk along this for 300m, and turn R to follow another signed footpath with a low wall and hedge immediately on your right-hand side. After walking the length of two fields you cross a stone stile into a third, and turn immediately R to follow the field boundary. Shortly turn L, and in a further 200m turn L again for a short distance. Cross the stile on your right into a field of pasture with the Pen Hill mast at its top.

Its correct name is the Mendip Transmitter, and although it belongs to the BBC, it is also used for HTV, Channel 4 and local radio stations. In addition it has attached to it several private communication aerials. The hilltop is 305m, or exactly 1,000 feet high and the mast is a further 314m tall, so that its top is over 2,000 feet above sea level. Made of tubular steel, it has a lift inside, to save the engineers a lengthy walk! Pen Hill, incidentally, is a tautological name, 'pen' being Celtic for hill.

The Right of Way continues straight ahead, eventually bearing R but always keeping close to the hedge on your left; however, after 600m or so (and having crossed a fence at a gate) you will see a grassy track veering slightly to the right, and it is easier to take this. Do not, however, go closer to the mast than this track. Either way, you will soon see a main road (the A39 from Bath to Wells and beyond), with an entrance gateway on your side and a small house on the other. This gateway is 6¾ km (4¼ miles) and 2 hours from the start, at GR 569488; turn R and immediately follow a metalled track going straight ahead. The main road bears off to the left of this track and although you get very close to it, you never set foot on the A39 itself.

The track you are walking is the route of the old road into Wells; the curve to the east taken by the present main road is an easing of the gradient made about 1830.

There is a sign to Pen Hill Farm, and a number of slightly intimidatory warnings, but do not worry; this track is a clear Right of Way and accepted as such. After 600m turn R, following the metalled track, into more open country. 100m further on you should bear L (downhill) rather than going into the strangely named 'Gollege'. Pass some woods on your left and proceed to, and straight past, Pen Hill Farm, continuing to go gently downhill. Make sure during this stretch that you frequently look down to your left, since from time to time you will get a glimpse of Wells Cathedral in the valley below; Glastonbury Tor is a more distant, but distinct landmark about 10 km (6 miles) away.

During this part of the walk you will have frequent glimpses of **Wells**. It may be England's smallest city, but it is rich in history. The old part of the town retains its medieval layout dominated by the cathedral church of St Andrew. (Be careful, however, not to confuse it with St Cuthbert's, Somerset's largest parish church, whose tower is slightly further to the west, a fine example of 15th-century Perpendicular architecture.) The cathedral is over 800 years old, replacing a church which tradition says was founded by King Ina of Wessex, at the suggestion of St Aldhelm, in 709. Nestling in quiet grounds next to the cathedral is the 14th-century Bishop's Palace with the famous bell-ringing swans on its moat.

Glastonbury Tor, the other feature on the horizon, has become the focus for a fine mixture of legends and Christian tradition. It is reputed to be the Isle of Avalon to which Arthur came to die, while Joseph of Arimathea is said to have hidden the Holy Grail in the rusty waters of Chalice Well, which rises at its foot. Some even believe that Christ himself walked here as a boy. In 1538, Richard Whiting, last Abbot of Glastonbury, was dragged to the top on a hurdle and there hanged, drawn and quartered. His crime? His gentle, almost pliant, nature gave Thomas Cromwell no reason to seize the Abbey for Henry VIII on grounds of treason, so he was accused of "robbery" and found guilty by a hand-picked jury. The tower at its summit is all that remains of a church built mainly in the 1330s but with the tower added in the 15th century. It replaced a church damaged in the earthquake of 1275. After the dissolution of the monasteries it gradually became a romantic ruin.

Archaeologists, historians and mystics rub shoulders at the Tor, as well as casual visitors. Besides the straightforward path to the top, there is the so-called 'processional way' which spirals around the hillside. On a clear day, when it simply looks like any other 'island' in the Somerset Levels, it is hard to understand quite why it should have the reputation it does, but when the levels are covered in mist and the Tor looms out of the white drift, it is easy to perceive it as the magic Isle of Avalon. It sits on a ley-line (for those who believe in them), the longest in England, stretching from Land's End to Bury St Edmunds.

Our path is more certain. One field, and about 400m, beyond the farm you will come to the corner of several fields. At this point the Right of Way turns sharp R, uphill along the edge of a field with a hedge on the left; at the next corner turn L along a track on the far side of (above) the hedge. Follow the track westwards, initially flat but then going downhill, past Ivy Cottage to a minor road. Cross this, go through a gate almost immediately opposite and bear L, following a footpath sign, diagonally and quite steeply downhill to the far bottom corner of the field.

At this point, going through a gate, you will find a track leading ahead. Do not take this, but veer slightly R of it into the woodland. Initially the track is not clear, but it improves as you continue. You should follow the small stream, or (in dry weather) the line it would take, downhill; you may cross the stream several times in seeking the easiest line, but this does not matter. After 350m from the gate you will see a stile leading into a small field: this is on the left of the stream. Cross this stile and walk through the field (bearing R) to a gate on to a minor lane only 80m away.

Here, if you are late or tired, you could turn R along this lane, which becomes a minor road and brings you, in just over 1 km (under ³⁄₄ mile) to the village of Wookey Hole (where you turn R for 200m to the lunch stop). By doing this, you would reach the pub in 20 to 25 minutes, saving about 15 minutes on the full route. But this would be a pity, for the next part of the walk is particularly interesting.

For the full route, cross the lane and go through the gate opposite. Do not walk down the drive (which is not a Right of Way), but instead walk downhill along the edge of the field keeping close to the hedge on your right. At the bottom there is a gate into an orchard. Go through this, across the orchard, through another gate, bear slightly L and make for the right-hand corner of the nearby buildings. (Don't worry, this is all a Right of Way!) At the corner you will find a kissing gate. Go through this, bear slightly L again and head uphill making for the left-hand edge of the extensive woods above you. At this corner, 300m from the kissing gate, there is another gate, though you will not see it until you are nearly there. Go through this and turn very sharply R to follow a path back along the top edge of the field you have just crossed, but just inside the woods. (Please do not attempt any short cuts across this field, but stick to the Rights of Way that we have described.)

200m along this track you will notice an old gate on your right, and a track bearing L. Take this track. It leads through the prominent gash in the hill (Milton Hill) which you will surely have noticed, and been intrigued about, for the last 15 minutes. As you go through you will realise that it is artificial, an old quarry in fact, but it is interesting to see how different are the rocks on each side of the path. (Do not be tempted to get too close, let alone to start climbing, as the cliff faces are very unstable.)

This quarry was finally closed about 1948 by which time concern was already being voiced about the damage to the environment, a debate which continues even more vigorously today. It was not the only quarry eating away at **Milton Hill**; slightly to the south-east was another and much larger one called Underwood Quarry (you do not pass it directly on this route, though you are very close to it). In 1895, the owners attempted to close the Right of Way which you will shortly be joining, but the people of Wells marched up the path to the music of the town band and smashed down the barriers. The path has remained open ever since, and has outlived both quarries, for Underwood closed in 1984. Today **Milton Hill Quarry** is a peaceful place. When you finally leave the quarry, watch out for the lime-kilns on the left before taking the route to Wookey Hole. Lime was used as a fertiliser of the land in the late 18th century, as parts of Mendip became enclosed and converted to fields. The natural stone had to be burnt to produce the pure lime. The great agricultural reformer Billingsley, writing in 1794, describes the Mendip limekilns as being "in the form of a French bottle".

Stick to the path and go slightly downhill to a small triangle of tracks, where you follow round, and down, bearing to the R. (But if you prefer a picnic to a pub lunch, then the large, flat grassy area on your left after you have gone through the narrow defile may well appeal.) At this point you cross the West Mendip Way, which we shall abbreviate WMW and which you will very soon rejoin to follow, with a minor variation, all the way to Priddy.

40

For more information about the Way see the description of Walk 1 on page 26.

After 150m from the triangle, go through a kissing gate on your R and follow the path downwards, keeping close to the hedge on your left for another 200m (it would not matter much if you stayed on the track for this stretch, as it will bring you to the same point). After a very short descent bear R, pick up the WMW and walk down the track keeping a wall on your left. This continues along the edge of a field (with a high hedge on your left) to a kissing gate and gate leading onto a road at the edge of the village of Wookey Hole. Turn R and follow this road (do not turn right again along Milton Lane) for 250m to the Wookey Hole Inn (on the right) and a welcome break for lunch.

On your way notice the **Stores & Post Office** (opposite the Village Club) said to date from the early 18th century, and, just before the pub, **The Chilterns**, now three cottages but once the mill manager's house and built in the late 18th century.

Although there are some old cottages, much of the village of **Wookey** dates from about 1850, when the Hodgkinson family acquired the paper mills, of which there are records from before 1610. During the 17th and 18th centuries, paper-making was a small-scale industry, but under the new owners, the mill expanded considerably, boosted by Gladstone lifting the duty on paper in 1861. The factory specialised in high-quality hand-made paper which was used for bank notes and indentures as well as drawing. Today, now managed by Madame Tussaud's, the mill is once again producing hand-made rag paper. The company also runs **Wookey Hole Caves** and **Lady Bangor's Fairground Collection**; they are to be congratulated on making a major tourist attraction fit so happily into a village, unlike the tawdry delights of Cheddar Gorge.

After lunch leave the inn, turn R and follow the road past the large car park for the caves, the paper mill and the entrance to the caves themselves.

Wookey Hole is another tautological name since 'Wookey' comes from the Celtic 'oguf' - a cave. Inhabited since 250BC, it was abandoned c.400AD but has attracted visitors ever since. The first account dates from 189AD, when Clement of Alexandria described a cave making the sound of clashing cymbals, a phenomenon caused by the movement of air and water in the many passages. Some visitors, like Celia Fiennes in 1698, were impressed, though she is faintly scornful of the way in which people detected resemblances between the formations and other objects, most famously the Witch of Wookey. Cynical old Daniel Defoe,

41

however, found "nothing of wonder or curiosity in it" and dismissed legends of the Witch as "fabulous and worth no notice". Alexander Pope came to remove "petrefactions" from the cave for his grotto at Twickenham, and it is suggested that Coleridge actually had in mind the River Axe at Wookey Hole as he wrote the lines:

> *Where Alph, the sacred river, ran,*
> *through caverns measureless to man .*

The escape of the River Axe from a picture by Michael Angelo Rooker of 1794

By the end of the 19th century, cave exploration became more scientific and pioneers such as Boyd Dawkins and Herbert Balch made discoveries here, furthering our knowledge of the past. Modern archaeologists continue their studies, working with teams of cave divers, participants in a sophisticated sport now centred on Wookey Hole.

Almost opposite the path to the caves you will find Bubwith Farm, dating from the early 15th century, when Bishop Bubwith owned the farm and caves, which on his death passed to the trustees of the Bubwith almshouses in Wells. Their tenant farmer was the custodian of the caves. Finally, don't miss the old road sign referring to charabancs. For those too young to remember, this was the name for motor coaches.

You stay on the road for only about 500m, but it seems to take longer than you might expect. Eventually, and after you have left the village, you will find a gate on your R with a WMW marker signed "Priddy". Go through the gate and follow the clear (but often muddy) route for about 600m, staying all the time near the foot of the valley. You then come to a gate leading into the Ebbor Gorge reserve, marked by several signs.

The reserve was given by Mrs G. W. Hodgkinson to the National Trust in 1967, in memory of Winston Churchill. It is a National Nature Reserve run by the Nature Conservancy Council. Some purists are disdainful of the way in which nature has been 'tidied up', but a successful nature reserve has to be managed, and it provides a safe home for a wide variety of wildlife, including trees and some rare wild flowers.

The WMW is indicated as going steeply up to the right. You will meet it again in less than a quarter of an hour, but in the meantime it is much more interesting to take the path through Ebbor Gorge itself; so go through the gate and bear R, following the clear (and initially level) path. Ebbor Gorge is less well known, but far finer than Cheddar Gorge - for one thing, it is far too narrow to be spoilt by a road! The path starts to climb, slowly at first, then more steeply as the gorge narrows:

> But the valley grew narrow and narrower still,
>   And the evening got darker and colder,
> Till (merely from nervousness, not from goodwill)
>   They marched along shoulder to shoulder.
>   (from The Hunting of the Snark *by Lewis Carroll*)

But you will find that even shoulder to shoulder becomes impossible, and single file is the only way up through the rocks. If you are unfamiliar with such terrain you may doubt that there is a route through, but have courage! The path involves a slight scramble (that is to say, you may sometimes need to support your progress by holding on with your hands), but is quite simple. We would however add that you should be careful of your footholds if it has been wet, as the rock is quite smooth and slippery.

Suddenly, after the steepest section, the path flattens out. Just pause here and look back, if necessary retracing your steps a few paces (but not down the steep rock steps), for a superb view of the gorge and the country beyond. It really is worth doing this, for while climbing you will have been looking at the rocks and not the view! When you are ready to continue, it is barely 100m to a T-junction of paths. Turn R (signposted to the car park) slightly uphill to another junction of paths in only 60m. Here the car park is signed right (and if you wish, you could go in that direction for a couple of minutes to a viewpoint, before returning to the junction). The path ahead descends quite steeply but you want to turn L, taking the only uphill path. After 250m you emerge from the trees and then reach a gate, stile and WMW marker (the WMW actually came up past the viewpoint just mentioned). Cross the stile and go ahead, keeping beside a fence on your left and bearing round with the fence to the L as well. At the gap ahead keep straight on (ignoring the clear track to the right) for 400m to Higher Pitts Farm.

As you are on the WMW you will find the route through the farm clearly marked. You go through a gate and slightly downhill towards another gate; just before this, turn L through a small gate to follow a narrow pedestrian track which turns R, below the obviously new house on your left, and emerges on to the main farm drive.

On your right you will see the farm buildings, once miners' cottages and the last relic of attempts to extract minerals from this part of the hills. The first company to open a pit here was the **Little Down and Ebbor Rocks Mineral Mining Company**, in 1856. They were looking for red ochre and the manganese mineral pyrolusite. The company failed, but in 1890 a second attempt was made, this time by the **Somersetshire Manganese and Iron Ore Company**. It lasted a year. Yet despite these failures, there are some rare minerals to be found here, including that confined to this area, Mendipite.

Take the farm drive for 150m to a T-junction, turn L and go straight on (the drive goes off to the right. You are now, in fact, once again on Dursdon Drove which you used early on in the walk. The Drove is first flat, then slightly downhill and you keep on it for 600m before bearing R, still following the WMW signs for Priddy, over a stile. For a short distance your path is fenced on both sides, so you cannot go wrong! You come to a R turn, and then in another 150m make sure that you cross the wall on your left by the stile. You then continue in the same direction, but on the other side of the wall, for about 200m, crossing one stile on the way. At the next field corner you turn L to follow the edge of the field (this is not marked, but it is clear that you should not cross any of the walls or hedges at this corner). A further 400m, passing a large depression containing a swallet entrance on your left, will bring you to a minor road. Turn R and walk for ³/₄ km (½ mile) into the centre of Priddy, bearing L at the first road junction; you may get some gentle amusement from some of the house names along here.

There are two pubs in **Priddy**, though they may well not be open when you come through. The first is the *Queen Victoria*, originally just the *Victoria Inn*. The building is about 250 years old, and was once a farm-house, as was the other pub. This, on your left as you come to the village green, is the *New Inn*. Like many of this ilk, it is no such thing, dating back to 1477. Almost opposite is **No 1, Pincross**, noteworthy for the inscription which is thought to have been by the builder. Clearly he was determined that his name should not be forgotten! To keep his ghost on our side, let us remind you - he was called Thomas Reeves.

On the large, triangular village green you will see a thatched pile of what look like elderly deck-chairs but are sheep hurdles. Since 1348 there has been an annual sheep fair here, held on the nearest Wednesday to 21st August. Some believe it moved here from Wells to avoid the Black Death. Certainly the date is right, and Priddy, the only village actually on the high Mendip plateau, would have been much healthier than low-lying, marshy, Wells. Others, however, suggest that the Carthusians, with their Mendip hill-farms, were responsible, and the date does appear to have religious connotations, being close to St Laurence's Day, the saint to whom Priddy's church is dedicated: to be precise, 10 days on, which looks suspiciously like a deviation due to the calendar change of 1752. Tradition has it that as long as the hurdles remain, so too will the fair. In the past, the influx of traders, tinkers, pedlars and entertainers must have made an already rough area even more violent. Today the scene is peaceful, with the **Manor Farm** buildings on the far side of the green adding to the attractive setting.

Here you finally bid adieu to the WMW which turns left by the New Inn and heads west towards Draycott and Cheddar; however you keep straight on (the right-hand of the two roads), keeping the green on your left, and walking towards the church which is your next objective. About 300m from the New Inn there is a house on the right called Solomon's Combe just before a lane bearing R which you take. Watch out for the relic of an earlier water supply.

Follow the lane round to the R to pass some low school buildings on your right and the school itself on your left with the church behind it.

St Laurence's Church almost resembles an outcrop of stone as it stands sturdily defying the cold winds which sweep across these hills. It has a Norman font, but its chief treasure is an ancient altar frontal, preserved in a glass case. It also has a charming modern memorial window, which portrays St Francis. The school stands near the church: Priddy children must be hardy if they take their breaks in the playground during the winter.

Cross the stone stile ahead and keep going, as near as possible, in the same direction. You are aiming for the Pen Hill mast (assuming it is visible), but you must lose height and gain it again. As you come over the brow of the hill you will see your intermediate target, the far corner of the field below you and (probably) somewhat to your left. Make for this corner, crossing a well used track just before you reach it (ignore this; it is a permissive path, only for the use of cavers visiting the nearby Swildon's Hole Cavern).

The cavern's popularity, evident from the state of the path, is because it is Mendip's most extensive and interesting cave. There are various entrances other than the one to the east of the church, such as in front of the *Victoria Inn* and on Priddy Green itself. There are about five miles of passages in a vertical range of 500 feet. The names of some of its features, such as Sore Knees Creep, Double Trouble series, Abandon Hope, and Paradise Regained, give an indication of its complexities. A stream flows into it, one of the sources of the River Axe, which disgorges from the hills at Wookey Hole, suggesting that the two sets of caves may join up, though no-one has yet made the breakthrough. Despite the cave's popularity, it can be dangerous, being prone to rapid flooding.

At the corner you cross two stiles (one wooden, one stone) and then head back uphill, again keeping to the same line, slightly left of the end of the line of trees. As you get closer you see a wall blocking your way; closer still and you observe a stone stile in this wall to the right of a gate. Cross this stile (perhaps with difficulty, for it is very high) and bear slightly L to walk along the left-hand edge of the next field. After 250m there is a further stile in the far corner, which you cross. (At the time of writing this was reduced to a gap in the wall.) Here you bear R towards the mast, and head for a ladder over the short stretch of wall that faces you.Cross this and go through the next field of rather damp pasture, keeping fairly close to the wall on the left. Again at the far end, you will see another stile (with a waymark) beneath two large trees and leading into a small caravan site. Cross this and go through the site, bearing somewhat R, to emerge onto a lane, Eastwater Lane. Here you are 6¾ km (4¼ miles) and 2¼ hours from Wookey Hole, at GR 537508.

At this point you are only just over half an hour from the end of the walk. If you would like to extend it, and particularly if you have an interest in tumuli, we describe at the end of this chapter an alternative route which is likely to take about 1¼ hours. But it is a very indirect way back! It has to be, because the Rights of Way do not enable you to take any of the apparently handy short cuts.

Turn R along the lane (another of Mendip's many drove roads), and after only 50m go through a gate on your left. The footpath goes diagonally R across the field, initially staying fairly close to the lane. You pass a caver's hut on your right and, after crossing a stile, the entrance to the cave (Eastwater Cavern) on your left. Veer very slightly L and make for the woods ahead; as you get closer you will see a stile and public footpath sign in front of you. Cross the stile onto a road, and turn L. Almost immediately, on your right, you may recognise the stile which you took this morning, about 25 minutes into the walk. You could now, of course, retrace your steps. We will however describe a slight variant – one which is easier to follow in this direction!

From the point where you joined the road and turned L, walk for 200m passing some cottages. After the third of these, turn L up the drive leading to Underbarrow Farm. Very soon the drive bears right and is clearly marked "No Right of Way", so you must make what seems a pointless diversion through the grounds of the small house ahead. Go ahead, passing the buildings on your left, and making very soon (less than 50m) for the right-hand corner of these grounds. Cross the stile and re-emerge onto the drive which you now cross to another stile almost opposite. Cross this and turn L, to follow a narrow but clear path in some light trees. After just under 400m you will reach a junction where a wider track comes in from the right.

While you stop to check your bearings you may notice a small pool to your right. This is **Fair Lady Well**, and although it is rather insignificant compared with the larger reservoirs, it is of some importance. It was the boundary marker between Priddy and Chewton Mineries, decided on in 1296, and even today it marks the parish boundary, which the 1:25,000 OS map will confirm for you.

Bear L here; you are now back on your outward route, and it is only 700m (less than half a mile) to the road at Stockhill Woods. When you reach this you will see the entrance to the car park opposite and slightly R. All that remains is for you to remember exactly where in the woods you left your car! (The afternoon walk is 8¾ km or 5½ miles, and should take about 2¾ hours.)

The Great Swallet of Eastwater drawn by Herbert Balch in 1913

For the extended version of the walk, turn L instead of R along Eastwater Lane. The metalled surface degenerates into a track, initially quite firm but later on it can be damp and muddy.

From here on it is known as Eastwater Drove. You have already met some of these drove roads, which were old routes used for driving animals to market. The great attraction was that they were free, unlike the 18th-century turnpike roads, although they were not kept in repair by the authorities. Even today, this particular track owes its present relatively good condition to the local farmer putting down hard-core. A large number of drove roads lead to Priddy, almost certainly because of the fair.

You walk along this track for just over a kilometre (nearly ¾ mile) until you reach another metalled lane, known as Nine Barrows Lane. Immediately you reach it, there is a gate and stile on your R, which you cross. Proceed diagonally L across the field. As you cross the brow of the slight rise, you will see woods ahead, and your objective is the far corner of these where there is (as you will see as you get closer) a gate. Having reached the gate, if you are not going to look at the circles, turn sharp R to go back across the field, this time making straight for the tumuli. (This erratic route is necessary to avoid leaving the Rights of Way.) However, if you want to take a quick look at Priddy Circles, you should go through the gate and cross the road to peer over the wall, before returning to the gate to follow the next part of the route.

In the field you should be able to see a curved bank extending into the adjacent field and enclosing a circle about 200m in diameter. This is the first of the strange earthworks known as **Priddy Circles.** They have been dated to about 2500 BC. Four remain, one rather damaged, and it seems likely there was another, between the third and fourth. There is certainly room for it, but during the Roman occupation a road was built to carry lead from the works at Charterhouse to other parts of Roman Britain. The circle was in the way, so it was simply swept away. The purpose of the circles is not known, beyond that it was almost certainly a ceremonial site. Each had a bank and ditch with a funnel-shaped entrance. There are other circles in the area: the one called Gorsey Bigbury between Charterhouse and Tyning's Farm, and another near Hunter's Lodge Inn.

Now return to the gate where you will go straight across the field.

There are two sets of *tumuli* in this field, which the OS map 1198 has misidentified. The first, of which there are eight, are Ashen Hill Barrows, the second set being the better known Priddy Nine Barrows. They are, like most on Mendip, round barrows, of the Bronze Age period. In fact, there are about 300 of this kind in the area, but this is certainly the most spectacular grouping. The Rev John Skinner, rector of Camerton, excavated them in 1815, selling his finds to raise money for his little church.

On reaching the tumuli, continue in the same direction (south) making for the left-most of the second set of barrows. Cross a stile and continue until you meet a wall (on the other side of which are the Priddy Nine Barrows). Veer L to follow this wall, without crossing it, over the top of North Hill and down the other side for nearly a kilometre (over ½ mile) towards a pool. Just before this, you meet a track; you need to turn sharp L to pick up the last 700m of the walk as described above.

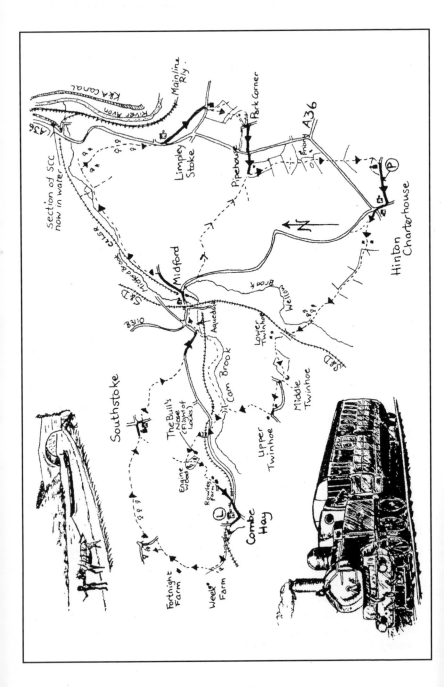

Section of SCC now in water

K&A Canal

River Avon

A36

Mainline Rly.

Park Corner

Priory

A36

Limpley Stoke

Pipehouse

Hinton Charterhouse

N

Midford Brook

Midford

C&LSRly

Wellow Brook

Lower Twinhoe

Middle Twinhoe

Upper Twinhoe

S&DRly

Southstoke

Aqueduct

Cam Brook

The Bull's Nose (Flight of Locks)

Engine Wood

Rowley Farm

Combe Hay

Fortnight Farm

Week Farm

3   Trains and Boats and Planes

Location	8 km (5 miles) south of Bath
Distance	6 km (3³/₄ miles) before lunch 11¹/₂ km (7¹/₄ miles) after lunch
Time	2 hours before lunch 3¹/₂ hours after lunch

Maps	Landranger 172 (Bristol & Bath)
	Pathfinder 1183 (Bath and Keynsham)
	   and either (former) 1199 (Radstock and Wellow)
	   or Explorer 5 (Mendip Hills East)

Start	Green Lane, Hinton Charterhouse (GR 776582)
Lunch	*The Wheatsheaf* at Combe Hay (GR 736601) Tel: 01225 833504

The starting point for this walk is by the church in Hinton Charterhouse, about 8km (5 miles) south of Bath. If coming from Bath take the B3110 (signposted to Frome). On reaching Hinton Charterhouse, turn L immediately after the Rose & Crown pub on the left, down Green Lane. After 400m (¹/₄ mile), and before reaching the small group of houses by the church, you should park on the left-hand side of the lane, beside a wall. (There is a little parking by the church itself, but we advise you not to use this in case it is required for church business.)

*   One of the features of this walk is a tunnel under an old railway, which you will encounter just after lunch. In normal conditions this presents no problem, but if it has been very wet recently you may well find the path through the tunnel flowing with water. Also, if you do the walk in gloomy weather, take a torch for this stretch, if you have one!*

The village of **Hinton Charterhouse** derives its name from the 13th-century priory whose ruins you will see in the latter part of the walk. However, right at the starting point, you may have noticed the Norman church of **St John the Baptist**, and through a gateway, across the fields to your right as you set out, can be seen **Hinton House**, dating from 1701. We will look at these more closely on our return.

On leaving your car you should walk back along Green Lane towards the Hinton Charterhouse. (Yes; you could have parked nearer the village, but you would not have saved any walking, for you will return to the church at the end.) Turn R past the Rose & Crown, walk along the B3110 for 150m and turn L after another pub, the Stag Inn (down a lane signposted to Wellow). Bear R immediately down a lane which becomes somewhat sunken, between high hedges; continue down this lane (ignoring footpath signs leading off) for 400m until you come to two houses. Pass between them, and go through a gate into a field.

*For the next kilometre or so (nearly ³/₄ mile) you follow the foot of the valley downwards, passing through three fields in all. The path is not always clear, but if in doubt follow fairly close to the stream, keeping it on your right. In the third field the route twists and turns a little; you will then come to a gate leading into a small wood. Go through this and follow the path which soon crosses the stream (to the R) by a plank bridge. After about 125m in the wood you recross the stream and cross a much more significant watercourse, the **Wellow Brook**, by a new and rather functional footbridge.*

On one bank of the stream you will notice a **Second World War pill box**. There are many in this area, although quite why it was felt necessary to defend these pretty valleys so strongly is rather a mystery. Some (where landowners were dilatory in demolishing them) are now being listed as structures of historic interest.

Turn R and follow the left bank of this brook for a short distance, then bear L away from the stream to two nearby gates. Go through the one ahead, and upwards to follow the track through an archway under a disused railway.

This is the line of the **Somerset & Dorset Railway,** sometimes called, rather unkindly, the "Slow and Dirty". This nickname seems to have been fostered by the Great Western Railway (which was no doubt prouder of its own nickname, "God's Wonderful Railway"), in order to discredit the S&D. In an attempt to alleviate their financial problems, the latter company had decided, in 1873, to extend their line from Evercreech Junction to Bath. They joined forces with the Midland Railway, using their station at Green Park in Bath, giving the Midland access to the South over standard gauge lines, which the GWR had been trying to prevent. This pretty route finally fell to the Beeching axe in 1966. You will meet the S&D again later, but in the meantime, try to imagine the Pines Express, pulled by *Evening Star*, thundering along through this quiet valley. About 50m after the archway you will cross the route of an old tramway. Intended to be a makeshift arrangement while the Radstock arm of the

Somersetshire Coal Canal was being constructed, it became permanent and eventually the whole arm was converted to tramway. The canal basin, where water met rail, was just to the west of where you are now. We will meet more definite traces of this canal later.

After this the track climbs steeply for a short distance. Some 125m from the railway you reach a house; just before this you must turn sharp L by a signed Public Footpath along a clear track. Almost immediately there are two gates ahead; make sure you take the right-hand one to stay on the track. Follow this for 250m until the ground levels out and you come to a stile and gap in the hedge. Here you must veer R, crossing the field diagonally and aiming just right of the buildings ahead. Go to, and through a gate (not over the stile a bit to the right, which is marked "Private"). Bear slightly L and, keeping just right of the stables in front of you, head for a stile and gate. Cross, turn R and keep on down the drive until you come to a minor road. [You may care to note that the Right of Way in the vicinity of the house and stables has been moved slightly from that shown on the OS maps.]

Turn R and immediately L following a Public Footpath sign, and cross the field towards its far right-hand corner (aim for the rightmost building). Just before the corner there is a stile on your right; cross this and go ahead keeping close to the edge of the field on your left. Ahead there is a small area of concreted farmyard; ignore this and pass just to the right of the farm buildings, and then out through a gate on your L onto the road. Turn R out of the gate. After 100m you reach Upper Twinhoe Farm, 3½ km (2¼ miles) and 1¼ hours from the start (at GR 748596).

Twinhoe appears as Twinney on maps as late as the 1870s, but it has reverted to a closer form of its original name, Twynyho. **Dr** Tunstall, who, in the 19th century, wrote a book of rambles around Bath, says it is a Celtic word meaning 'the land of little hills', and after this walk, you may well think he is right.

At Upper Twinhoe Farm turn R down a clear, signed bridleway. Some 300m later, do not go through the gate ahead, but turn L; the track becomes a path. For a while you are going downhill twisting and turning, on a sunken path enclosed with shrubs and trees. This is a good place for uliginose plants! If it has rained recently, the path will seem more like a stream but the surface is firm and you should not have much trouble. At the foot of the wood you emerge in the valley of the Cam Brook, ahead, which you cross; the footbridge is quite solid, but the path on each side of it can be muddy. About 50m after the bridge you should see, on your right, a stile and path waymarked as the Limestone Link. Do not take this; but only a few paces further on, the Limestone Link is also marked, less distinctly, as turning L over a stile into woodland. This path you do want to take.

If you have done the first walk in this book, you have already met the **Limestone Link** which, as its name suggests, links two other routes, the **Cotswold Way** and the **West Mendip Way** (although not end to end). Slowly, more and more of these link paths are being constructed to connect existing long distance footpaths, giving keen walkers the opportunity to travel very long distances by paths and tracks. However, the track by which you descended from Upper Twinhoe is rather older, being a pack route; many of these find their way across these valleys, leading from Bath by a variety of routes to destinations such as Salisbury.

Follow this Link path, crossing an obviously artificial construction which is, in fact, a former lock (now filled in) on the Somersetshire Coal Canal, to a stile. You then pass some corrugated iron sheds on your right, and cross two more stiles (each beside a gate). At the second, which is beside Bridge Farm, you emerge onto a minor road (at GR 745604).

The next part of the walk follows the course of a 'ladder of locks' on the Somersetshire Coal Canal. The idea for this canal was first mooted in 1792, when the owners of the Somerset coalfields were seeking means of supplying their coal more cheaply to Bath and Bristol, to compete with imports from Wales and the Midlands. With news of the plans for a Western Canal (later to be called the **Kennet & Avon Canal**) surveys were undertaken by **John Rennie**, engineer on the K&A. Royal Assent for the two canals was obtained on the same day in 1794, and work began a year later. Two arms were planned for the Coal Canal: the main route was to run from the **Dundas Aqueduct** on the K&A through to Paulton; the other branched off at Midford and was to go to Radstock. Problems immediately arose, these being, as they so often were with canals, hills and water. As you have already discovered, delay in building locks on the Radstock arm meant there had to be a tramway over part of it, purely as a temporary measure, of course. The locks never were built, and although the rest of this branch was once in water, and boats even travelled on it regularly, the inconvenience of trans-shipping brought about the change to a complete tramway after just a few years.

On the other arm, the builders were confronted with a steep climb to **Combe Hay**. Anxious to avoid a long flight of locks, which take a lot of building and waste water, or tunnelling right through the hill, the directors sought a more drastic solution. The fashionable idea at the time was a caisson lock, a large box into which the narrow boat would float. Doors at each end were closed, and the box rose or sank in a brick-lined chamber, to take it to the required level, when the doors opened again, and the boat floated out. One designer of such a lock was **Robert Weldon**, who demonstrated his invention to some members of the K&A Committee. They were considering the possibility of using it at Devizes, but cannily persuaded the SCC committee to try it out on their canal first, paying a quarter of the costs. It was a wise decision. At first all seemed well. The lock became quite a tourist attraction, and the final accolade came when, despite poor weather, the Prince of Wales spent a happy hour or two there. Legend has it that it was with difficulty he was restrained from actually travelling in it. However, the account of his visit mentions the slippery state of the soil. This was possibly caused by the clayey nature of the soil, which contained fuller's earth, and it was this that proved the lock's downfall. The clay retained water, causing the sides of the chamber to bulge and the lift to jam. The lock was abandoned in favour of an inclined plane, yet even after its demise it had its attractions. **Jane Austen** came with her uncle Leigh Perrott to see it as late as 1801.

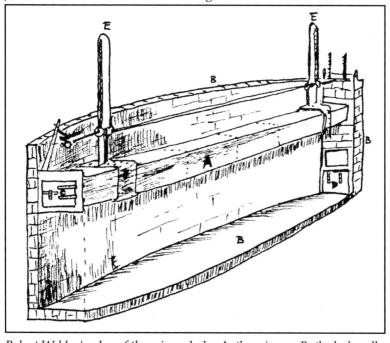

Robert Weldon's plan of the caisson lock - A: the caisson; B: the lock walls; C: entrance door in the caisson; D: exit to the canal; E: lifting mechanism

A feeder canal ran to the base of the inclined plane, the split occurring roughly where you are now standing. The plane then ran straight up the hillside, rejoining the canal near **Caisson House**. Wagons carrying three boxes each with a ton of coal were linked to an endless chain which ran around cylindrical wheels at top and bottom. The weight of the descending wagons carried the empty wagons back to the top, this system being known as a Whimzey or a Jenny. It was not a success and was replaced by 'The Bull's Nose', the flight of locks you are now about to see. To reach this you will pass under another old railway and in doing so you will discover a useful display panel on the wall of the arch beneath which you pass. This gives a good explanation of the locks, and as you climb past them, try to imagine life nearly 200 years ago, when loaded coal barges came down here. There was difficulty, not least rounding the corner which forms the bull's nose and there was danger: one young boy working on a barge drowned here. Yet on a fine summer's day, it must have seemed there were much worse ways of earning a living.

Cross the road, go under the old railway arch (where you find the display panel on your right), and follow the track over the stile by the gate. (Initially you keep as much to the right as you can, with a high bank on your right.) As you go, there are the remains of several locks on your left. After about 250m you pass a stile at a gap, and then in another 150m, you come to a gate and stile. Do not cross these; instead, turn L, cross the tiny stream by a plank bridge and climb steeply upwards to the L. This climb in the woods can be awkward, as the ground is slippery, but it is fairly short. (At the gate and stile the Limestone Link goes ahead; you leave it for a short while, but will rejoin it.)

This is called Engine Wood, after the pumping engine used to pump water back from the bottom of the flight to the reservoir at the top. A feeder canal (besides which you will soon find yourself) led from the old basin at the top of the inclined plane along to the pump. The strange bits of brickwork that you pass as you reach the top are remnants of the engine house. For those who are enthusiastic about such things, it was a Boulton and Watt single-action beam engine, with two wagon-top boilers. Despite the presence of the pump, there were still times when use of the flight was restricted due to lack of water.

You pass the low brickwork arch just mentioned and after a short distance cross a stile and turn R to cross the line of the feeder canal. Follow the clear footpath signs uphill across the field [note that at this point the Right of Way has been diverted from the line shown on the OS maps]. At the top of the field cross the stile and turn L, soon going through a gate and emerging onto a track leading past Rowley Farm, now converted into several large residences on the left, all with 'Rowley' in their names.

It is frustrating for canal enthusiasts that the footpath has been rerouted to avoid some of the most interesting parts of the SCC, but hoards of remnant-hunters were beginning to destroy the peace of those who live here. In particular, the mystery of the location of the caisson had seized people's imagination, and some indulged in unauthorised excavations to try out their theories. During the next part of the walk, however, you can see traces of the summit level of the canal, but it has become rather tangled up with the **Camerton and Limpley Stoke Railway** (C&LSR), whose history you may like to consider over lunch.

Emerging onto the farm drive, you follow this ahead and down, crossing the old railway at a point where it entered a short tunnel, and immediately coming to a minor road. Bear R and in less than 200m you will see, above you on your right, the Wheatsheaf Inn at Combe Hay. Turn R and make the short climb to the bar, spurred on, no doubt, by the prospect of your lunch break here. (Combe Hay is 6 km or 3¾ miles from the start, at GR 736601. The morning walk might take you 2 hours, plus any time you have spent inspecting the industrial archaeology on the way.)

The Rise and Fall of the Railways: The first part of the SCC to fall to the railway was, unsurprisingly, the Radstock tramway. It must be said that the SCC had been an extremely successful canal, perhaps the most successful in the entire waterways system. In its heyday, investors had been paid dividends of up to 7%. However, slowly but surely the railway companies were making inroads on the canal trade. When the S&D decided to extend their line to Bath, the Canal Company saw that this would be in direct competition with the tramway, on which the motive power was still the horse. There was little doubt who would win. They therefore made the best of a bad job and sold the tramway to the S&D (to the disgust of the GWR). By 1893 the SCC was in liquidation, and so the GWR (who already owned the K&A) stepped in, with a proposal to lay a track along the line of the canal. Some alterations had to be made; embankments, viaducts, and cuttings were necessary here and there, but the line was completely open by 1910. One observer described the route as a "series of delights". Sadly, as the Somerset coalfields declined, so did the C&LSR, and it finally closed in 1951. However, by that time, it had become famous as the track on which *The Ghost Train* was filmed in 1931, and in 1952, after its official closure, it once again starred in a film, *The Titfield Thunderbolt*.

The run-down of the S&D began in 1958. The last Pines Express ran in 1962, and, as already mentioned, the line closed completely in 1966. Despite its inefficiency compared with rail or water, the internal combustion engine had triumphed.

————————————

After lunch, leave the pub through the car park and turn R going uphill on a minor lane. After barely 100m, take a track veering L and only a few paces further on, bear L downhill (at a very small waymark) to follow a footpath slanting down through the trees. Go down the steps and over a stile; when you emerge into the field, continue diagonally R and downhill, heading not for the gate in the right-hand corner but for a stile to its left that leads back into woodland. Cross this and make your way through the trees to a stream along a field edge. This stream you will have to cross at a convenient point, but you then continue upstream along it until you see, on your right, a low tunnel under the old railway. (The tunnel is only 200m from the last stile; this stretch is easier to walk than to explain! The entrance and exit may have low gates, to prevent animals wandering through, but these are easy to cross.) The stream flows through the tunnel, and your path turns R and goes through it too: it is a Right of Way! In normal conditions the raised flagstones enable you to avoid the water; if the stream is full this may not be the case, but it is not very deep.

This little tunnel is the **Combe Hay aqueduct**, possibly one of the most insignificant in existence! Clearly something has happened to it since it carried the canal, the something being the railway. The tunnel was widened (if you are not too busy keeping to the path in the tunnel, you may have time to notice that the construction of the roof varies) and an embankment was built on top. The flagstones were laid to confirm it as a Right of Way.

On emerging from the tunnel, follow the path ahead which is rising slowly, but staying in the valley bottom. Cross a stile and go on for 200m through a field to a farm gate with a stile on the left. Cross this, and turn R up the lane.

The farm on the hillside facing you as you came through the gate is **Week Farm**; further up the lane, on your left you will pass **Fortnight Farm**, and old maps show **Three Day Farm** down the lane in the direction of Combe Hay. Was this the frequency with which the farmers had to pay their rent, one wonders? Surely not every three days!

After 250m the lane veers R, and after the same distance again it once more veers R. At this second bend you veer L to leave the lane. The footpath you want (which should, but may not be marked) goes diagonally R across and up the field in a straight line to the far corner (which has trees on each side of it). The line goes past a pole carrying electricity supply cables. On reaching the corner, cross the gate and follow the track R for a short distance, to emerge on a road at a bend. Bear R.

You hardly set foot on the road before you turn R again through a new kissing gate and follow a marked footpath L across a small field [the Right of Way appears to have been moved slightly here] to pick up a clear path with open, flat country on your left and a steep slope down (partly tree-covered) on your right. This path becomes a track and then a drive and continues, almost straight, for about 1 km (under ¾ mile) until you approach some farm structures ahead. Just before these, there are more gates than we have ever seen in one place before! You must bear R, probably going through two of the gates, and then follow the drive, gently descending, round to the L. You are now approaching Southstoke village; as you near it, there is a junction with a drive downhill to the right, but you must keep L. Go ahead through a gate onto a road, with the church on your right. (Southstoke is 3 km, 2 miles and 1 hour from Combe Hay, at GR 747613.)

This is an attractive approach to **Southstoke**, passing as it does the church standing almost in the grounds of **Manor Farm**, which has a fine barn with a dovecote gable. These predate the farmhouse itself which is 17th-century. The church is dedicated to **St James the Great**; there is evidence of a Norman church, but most of it dates from the 15th century, though needless to say, the Victorians have had a hand in it. Despite being something of a dormitory village for Bath, Southstoke has retained a sense of identity, and contains some attractive buildings. Watch out for the **Packhorse Inn** a little further on along the route. This sounds as though it should be very old, and as a building it is, being 17th-century, but it has only been an inn since 1825, when this road was constructed to improve the old pack trail. (Before that the inn was at **Pack Horse Farm**.) The house replaced a previous one, and, in the 'waste not want not' style of building used in former times, almost certainly contains parts of the earlier home. Having been built before 1697, when Window Tax was introduced, the owners had been quite liberal with windows; you will notice that they smartly bricked up several once they had to pay duty on them.

The road ahead splits; you should take the R (lower) fork by the telephone box and after 50m turn R (downhill) for less than 100m. Shortly after you pass the

Packhorse Inn, on the right, you will see a footpath signed L alongside the wall of a row of cottages. Take this and quite soon, as you approach some gates leading to private grounds, bear R (again downhill). Initially the path is enclosed by walls and, although not very straight, is impossible to miss. In parts it may be muddy, for you are following the start of another stream, which feeds into the Cam Brook. After the first stile (at the end of a short stretch of woodland) you must take the path going down to the L, as close to the infant stream as you can. As the valley opens out you cross a number of stiles, always keeping near the stream. As the stream becomes more conspicuous you find yourself on its left, probably without being conscious of having crossed it.

Eventually, some 600m from Southstoke, you enter a larger field. About halfway through this field you will see, on your right, that the stream runs under a culvert, bearing left as it does so. Cross this culvert and continue ahead, with the stream now on your left. As you approach the few buildings of Upper Midford you must cross a couple of stiles (and, incidentally, the stream again) and emerge onto a drive which shortly joins a road. Go ahead on the road for 200m until it turns L (with a private drive to Hyver Kennels on the right). Just round this corner on the R a footpath sign leads you into another field which overlooks the Cam Brook. Your route is diagonally L across the conspicuous depression (the line of the old canal) to pick up a track (on the former tow-path) which heads towards some woodland; however you may first wish to go down (half right) across the dip to inspect the old canal bridge, for you have once again joined the SCC.

The house whose drive you passed is **Hyver Kennels**, and it is suggested that it was once a canal-side inn, *The Boatman's Arms*. This would make sense, for this was a particularly busy part of the canal, being close to the junction of the Radstock arm. It had a tow-path on each side here, which can still be seen, and the turnover bridge allowed crossing from each side. It also kept open a lane between Twinhoe and Midford. Now it sits rather forlornly in the field, having no purpose left in life. Turning back on to the route towards **Midford**, you will see on your right an impressive if somewhat ruinous bridge crossing the **Cam Brook**. This is the **Midford Aqueduct**, and here the Radstock arm turned south. On the other side of the brook was a complex series of wharfs, where boats trans-shipped cargo to or from the tramway, depending on whether it was goods coming in, or coal going out. Weather and neglect are slowly obliterating the inscription on the eastern face that tells us that R Tyler erected "Mitford Aqueduct, 1803". However, plans are in hand to conserve and protect what remains, and restoration work has already begun in this area. An example of this is on the other side of the brook, where there is what appears to be a little shelter built into the slope. This was a powder house, where gunpowder, used in coal-mining, could be stored. It has a strong, stone-vaulted roof covered in turf to absorb shock, should there be an explosion, and was restored in 1994.

As the path nears the trees (keeping some 50-75m away from the brook on your right) it again becomes rather twisty, but also clearer to follow. You pass a wire fence enclosing a garden, and under two bridges (one a road bridge, and the other from the former railway). The path then comes out on the road at Midford, which is 5 km (3¼ miles) and slightly over an hour and a half from Combe Hay, at GR 761607.

Before negotiating the traffic at Midford pause for a while to sort out the confusion of bridges here. Once upon a time there was just one of stone, which crossed the **Midford Brook**, formed from the Cam Brook and its vigorous neighbour, the Wellow Brook. Then the canal arrived, and another stone one had to be built to allow it to pass under the road at Midford, with a wooden one for Twinhoe Lane. Then along came the S&D, and with it a viaduct across the main road. Meanwhile, the wooden bridge in Twinhoe Lane was replaced by the iron one beneath which you walked. Midford Station was behind the *Hope and Anchor Pub*, and in 1936 it was the scene of considerable excitement when a runaway train smashed past the signal box and through the station. The trucks gave up at this point, but the engine, a type known as a Jinty, ran on nearly into Bath until derailed by debris from the one truck it was still towing. Finally the C&LSR arrived and their viaduct (which is down the road to your right) had to dodge and weave its way over the Midford Brook and the road, under the S&D, and over Twinhoe Lane. Even though partly dismantled, railway enthusiasts still find its convolutions of great interest.

Before crossing the road you will notice just next to the pub a driveway leading to a house called **Lynwood House**. (Please respect the privacy of the owners and do not walk down the drive.) It stands on the site of the SCC weigh-house. Here boats were checked in order to calculate tolls, many boat-owners not being above carrying undisclosed cargo. Although strictly utilitarian in purpose, it was built in the style of a Greek Temple crossed with a Tudor mansion.

After crossing the road and the brook, and as you reach your next junction, watch out for the milestone on the western side of the road. This rather elegant construction, telling you the distances to

Bath, Warminster and Frome, is typical of the stones erected by the Black Dog Turnpike Trust, who administered this stretch of highway. Before 1834, when the trust built the present A36, this was the main route to Warminster. The 'stone' is actually a metal plate attached to a real stone at the back.

The Somersetshire Coal Canal weigh-house at Midford - the dereliction years

Cross the road here and turn R. This is the B3110 (and is no doubt the road you used this morning to get to Hinton Charterhouse if you came from Bath); although only a B road it is busy, so take care as you walk along it. You do this for under 200m, crossing the Midford Brook and the old railway, and then you turn L along a much less important road called Midford Lane.

From Midford the full route is a further 6½ km (4 miles) and might take 2 hours. A short cut starts here, and will rejoin the main route 1½ km (1 mile) from the end; it will save 3 km (2 miles) and nearly an hour.

For the short cut do not turn L along Midford Lane, but continue on the B3110 for just over 100m. (It might be safer to recross to the right-hand side briefly, though you will then have to cross for a third time. The milestone is on the right just after Midford Lane.) As the road curves right you will see veering L a track going fairly steeply upwards, which you take. It is another old road, and for the next 1½ km (1 mile) you can hardly go wrong as it twists upwards between high banks. In places it is a bit of a scramble, but is nowhere difficult; if it has been very wet the track can be (like the one down from Upper Twinhoe Farm) more like a stream but the surface underfoot is firm.

After 600m the track turns R, and soon the slope eases and the views open up. Keep going until the track becomes surfaced at the edge of a small village called Pipehouse. Go ahead into the village; you pass on the left the former Village Room dated 1903, and then take a signed footpath R beside Ashleigh Cottage. When you turn R you rejoin the full route at the point marked ♦ below.

Midford acquired a castle in about 1775, and on the next stage of the full walk you should get good views of it on the hillside across the valley to your left. Built in the Gothick style, it is, you will notice, rather a strange shape. It was commissioned by **Henry Roebuck** (who sounds as though he comes straight from a Sheridan play) to commemorate a substantial win at the gaming table, or so the story goes. He built it in the shape of the winning card, the Ace of Clubs. It does seem to be the only explanation of its odd construction. Roebuck also built a 'priory' and a 'hermitage' to add to its picturesque nature: it looks suspiciously as though he bought up some unwanted parish church to import into his garden. You will see its tower beside the castle.

For the full route, go along Midford Lane, gaining a little height, for 300m and look out for a footpath sign on the L as the lane veers right. Follow this path (you hardly change direction at this point), initially on the level and then gradually descending back towards the embankment of the old railway. You reach this at some woods. Cross a stile and follow through the trees, first close to the embankment, then veering slightly R to follow close to the Midford Brook (on your left). From Midford bridges to where you rejoin the brook is 1 km (less than ³/₄ mile); you then go on for a further 550m to a junction of paths.

Continue straight ahead at the junction by crossing a couple of stiles (do not go over the footbridge). The path rises away from the brook, passing a large house above you. When, after about 300m, you reach the drive to that house, there is almost opposite you a stile and footpath leading up the field towards the wood. Take this path (your line is slightly L of straight up), over a stile into the wood, and continue climbing through the trees. The slope then eases. The path stays quite clear but at one point, about 250m from where you entered the trees, look out for, and take, a L fork. By now you are on the flat, and you come into rather more open country; then the path descends again, back into the woods. During this stretch you may notice that you actually pass part of a train, although how it arrived here we leave to your imagination. In another 500m you come down to a main road, the A36. Here you are 8 km (5 miles) and 2½ hours from Combe Hay, at GR 779610.

It is necessary to cross the A36 in order to take the old road which continues almost directly ahead of you, passing just right of the pub, the Rose & Crown. Traffic on the A36 comes round the bend to your left at a rapid pace, so we suggest that you walk on for a few metres before trying to cross. Having done so, bear R to take the lane just mentioned, called Middle Stoke . The walk along here through Limpley Stoke is likely to be as quiet as the A36 was noisy. Once on this lane there are no junctions for ³/₄ km (½ mile) and you walk on until you come to a T-junction and the church.

The A36 frequently has roadworks on it, as it has a distressing tendency to slide downhill. Since it came into existence in 1834, when it was built by the Black Dog Turnpike Trust for carriages and horse-drawn transport, one can well understand that modern traffic does it no good at all. The pub is the second **Rose & Crown** you have encountered today; it became a popular inn name in the 17th century, when it was deemed to indicate loyalty to Sovereign and Country (without specifying which sovereign - a wise precaution at that time!). This particular one was a house selling beer and cider and is thought to be 17th-century.

In 1876 Dr Tunstall described Limpley Stoke as "one of the most picturesque villages in the neighbourhood of the city. The houses are, for the most part, built with charming irregularity on the side of the hill." As you walk along the lane, you may feel that, with one or two exceptions, it has changed little over 120 years. The spring forming a little well on the right-hand side of the street was used until 1935. Many of the houses are weavers' cottages and date back to the 16th century. The little church of St Mary the Virgin is the oldest church you see on this walk, dating back to Saxon times. A quick look through the church door will show that although the porch is Norman, there is a simple Saxon arch retained within the interior structure of the building. The Saxons were not the earliest settlers here, however, for Roman remains have been found in the area. It seems that people have been taking pleasure in this valley for nearly 2,000 years.

At the church you bear R through a squeeze stile and take a path which passes to the right of the church and then crosses a stile into a field. In the field, continue on the line of the churchyard wall that you have just been following, going down slightly and then staying almost flat (there is a more prominent path going downwards to your left, which you do not want). Go through a kissing gate and continue ahead, making for a cottage whose roof and chimneys you have been able to see straight in front of you since leaving the church.

Pass through a kissing gate and veer R along a path which soon becomes a track which has gardens to its left and a field on the right; after 200m this track brings you to a lane. Turn L (downhill). Very soon you come, firstly, to a road going left and almost immediately afterwards another road going uphill R. Take this sharp R turn and walk up for 350m back to the A36. (You may have noticed in the village that your road was marked as a 'No Through Road'. At the top you will realise that it is only the very last bit that is 'one-way', to prevent traffic using this as a way out onto the main road.)

The part of **Freshford** through which you have just passed is called **Park Corner**, due to its proximity to the park-like grounds of the monastery at **Hinton Charterhouse**. You will be passing near to its remains in the concluding part of the walk.

*Here the A36 is much easier to cross, and you should have little difficulty in finding your way over and along the lane opposite for 200m to a little settlement called **Pipehouse** (thought to be a corruption of Pipards, a family name). Look out here for a footpath coming in from the right, and then immediately one going L, which you take. (♦ This is where you will rejoin the full route if you took the short cut from Midford; but then the footpath you want is a right turn, not a left.)*

The end is now 1.6 km (exactly 1 mile) away, and your last lap is across a number of fields and lots of stiles; the route is, of course, a Right of Way, though there is not always a clear path. Having turned L you cross the first few stiles and veer L to walk through a small field with a hedge on your right. At the other end of this field, go over the stile and veer just slightly R towards a stile ahead. (There is also a path towards the far left corner of this field. The stile you want is 60m to the right of this corner.) Cross this stile and veer R again, heading to the right of the buildings ahead.

The group of buildings marks the site of **Hinton Priory**, from which Hinton Charterhouse derives its name. Founded about 1230 by **Ela, Countess of Salisbury,** in memory of her husband, it was a Carthusian Priory, as the name Charterhouse suggests. Ela had turned to the religious life after her husband's tragic death, and also founded the Abbey of Lacock, of which she was abbess. Over the years it grew from the original simple chapel to be a power in the area. After disputes between the village and the priory, the monks actually took over the running of the church at Hinton Charterhouse itself: Freshford also belonged to the monks and **Friary Wood**, to the south-east, owes its name to the priory. There lived the lay brothers, beside the River Frome. The foundation seems to have been sufficiently wellknown for

Shakespeare, in his play *Henry VIII*, to refer to "Nicholas Henton ... a Chartreux friar". Today only the chapter-house and the refectory remain, for in the 16th century the buildings were plundered to provide material for the manor house standing close by. In the 1950s, excavations revealed the extent of the cloisters, some of the monks' dwellings and part of the church. Measurements taken at the time also proved that some of the stonework in the house would fit into the original monastic buildings. The large, and now very overgrown, ponds which you eventually pass on your right were possibly the fishponds.

Under the trees you will find yet another stile: cross this, go ahead to the next one quite soon and veer L to go along with a wall on your left and a copse on your right. After 175m you find your next stile. Cross this and bear noticeably R to cross the next, larger field (if you can see the church ahead, 3/4 km away, that is exactly the line you want). At the far side of that field, cross the road and go over another stile, continuing in the same direction. At this stage you may encounter one or two electric fences (and, if you are using the OS 1:25,000 maps, you will find field boundaries somewhat changed), but suitable crossing places are put on the line of the Right of Way. Head for the wood to the left of the church; the route passes a large, lone tree before you reach the wood. As you get nearer Hinton Charterhouse church, you will see Hinton House on your right.

Hinton House dates from the early 18th century, and its proximity to the church was reflected by the interest which its owners took in the life of the parish. There is a private gate from the grounds into the churchyard. One highly respected owner, Samuel Day, died a rather curious death in 1806. He went to Bridgwater to attend a parliamentary nomination and fell from the hustings, thus proving, one supposes, that politics are bad for your health. His son, who did not long outlive him, is described in the church history as a ne'er-do-well, but his monument in the church, erected by his grieving mother, unsurprisingly gives no indication of this.

You should, however, keep heading L of the church aiming for the trees. When you reach the trees, walk alongside them for a few paces, with them on your right, to find a small path signed R. Take this over stiles and through the trees into the churchyard.

The founding of the church, dedicated to St John the Baptist, predates the priory; two rather glum heads on each side of the inner door probably date from Norman times. The top part of the tower was rebuilt in 1770, and the two Bath architects, Thomas Jelly and John Palmer were responsible for the design. Thomas Hardy readers will be interested to know that there were church minstrels until 1850, when, like those in *Under the Greenwood Tree*, they were replaced by a church organ. The church is kept locked, but the key is not far away.

Go ahead through the churchyard and leave by the main gate to the left. Turn R and follow the lane round to the L for 50m to rejoin Green Lane where you started. If you parked as we advised, your car will be nearby on your right. By the full route, the afternoon walk is 11½ km (7¼ miles) and 3½ hours long.

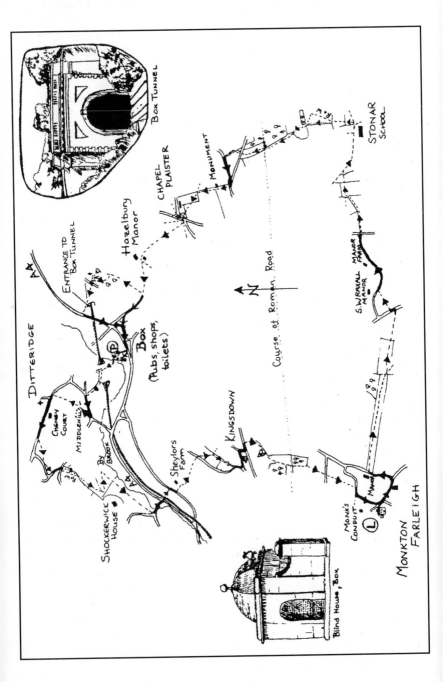

DITTERIDGE

Entrance to Box Tunnel

Hazelbury Manor

CHAPEL PLAISTER

MONUMENT

Box Tunnel

Chimney Court

MIDDLEHILL

By Brook

SHOCKERWICK HOUSE

Box
(Pubs, shops, toilets)

Sheylors Farm

KINGSDOWN

Course of Roman Road

N

S.W. RAYALL MANOR
MANOR FARM

STONAR SCHOOL

Monk's Conduit

MANOR

MONKTON FARLEIGH

Blind House, Box

4 Springs, Spas and Holes in the Ground

Location	West Wiltshire, about 11 km (7 miles) east-north-east of Bath
Distance	8 km (5 miles) before lunch 11¼ km (7 miles) after lunch
Time	2¼ hours before lunch 3¼ hours after lunch
Maps	Landranger 173 (Swindon & Devizes) Pathfinder 1184 (Melksham)
Start	Box recreation ground car park (GR 824686)
Lunch	*The King's Arms* at Monkton Farleigh (GR 804655) Tel: 01225 858705 (note that on Wednesdays the lunchtime menu, though quite adequate, is more restricted than on other days).

The starting point for this walk is in the village of Box, which from Bath is most easily reached by following the A4 eastwards towards Chippenham. Just after you come into Box there are some traffic lights; bear L following the A4. Almost immediately, turn L into a minor road called Valens Terrace which goes downhill (do not turn very sharp left towards the church). At the bottom of this road, on the right, is a large car park for the hall (Selwyn Hall) and recreation ground, and you can leave your car here.

Rather unusually, we suggest that you start this walk with a short detour, in order to visit Box Church which is particularly interesting. To do this, walk back up the road towards the A4, and at the top, turn sharp R down Church Lane. (If you do not wish to make this detour, then leave the car park by the gate where you entered it, turn sharp R to the foot of the road and then L after the last house of a terrace. Walk down a narrow track, with a light-coloured house on the right, for 125m to the footbridge over the By Brook. Cross this to pick up the route at the point marked ♦ in the next 'italic' paragraph.)

The pub on the corner of the lane, now called **Bayly's**, was once an inn or ale-house called **The Bear**. Its stables were across the road, and are now the premises of the local pharmacy. The present name comes from a family who were landlords in the 17th century, and who testified in a case brought by the ominously named Committee of Ejectors against the local vicar. A number of charges were brought against him, including drinking too much and "attempting to induce a woman to acts of uncleanliness", thus explaining the present inn sign. He was even accused of murdering a family friend. The true reason was that he was a Royalist; another charge gives it away: "expressing dissatisfaction with the government". The trial, despite its apparent disapproval of drinking, was held in several pubs,with a motley crew of witnesses assembled against him. The unfortunate vicar was, unsurprisingly, found guilty, though not of the charge shown on the inn sign. Lovers of justice will be pleased to know that he was restored to the living in 1660, with the return of the King.

As you walk down **Church Lane**, the first building you should look out for is a large 18th-century house on your left, called **Springfield**. It looks rather plain, and this is because in 1729 it was constructed as the **Poor House for Box and Ditteridge**, and contained a large room used as a Charity School. Some of the money for the venture was given by **Henry Hoare**, the 18th-century banker better known for his pleasure grounds at Stourhead. The church is on your left and if you have started early, it is well worth a visit. An excellent guidebook is available in the church, but to summarise briefly its history, it is dedicated to **St Thomas à Becket** and may date back to the Saxon period; certainly there was a Norman church here. The north wall of the chancel is the earliest part. In the 13th century the patronage of the church was given to the priory of Monkton Farleigh, a village we shall visit later on in the walk. The monks were already using a local mill. The 15th century saw the tower transformed from being short and squat into a more elegant form with a slender spire, and more substantial work was undertaken in the 18th century. Considerable rebuilding was undertaken, possibly made necessary by damp, and the Doric doorway was added, looking a little out of place on this Gothic church.

There are connections here with **Hazelbury**, which you will see on your way back to Box. Against the south wall are the graves of the **Speke** family, who owned Hazelbury in the 17th century, and three stone coffins leaning up against the west boundary wall are thought to have come from the original **Hazelbury Church**. While on the subject of coffins, there is an unusual carving on the south wall slightly to the west and above a blocked doorway. It is a little stone coffin or *memento mori*, to remind everyone that death is not far away. It was built into the wall in 1713, but is probably of earlier date.

Beyond the church to the west are the grounds of **Box House**, built about 1800 as the vicarage, after the old one was destroyed by fire. **Dr Isaac Horlock** had the money to construct this stylish house (now an hotel) from the income from his sugar estates in Jamaica. The Horlocks kept the living in the family, and a curious story attaches to Isaac's son, Holled Darrell Cave Smith Horlock (the family went in for impressive names). At dinner one evening, his wife and her sister were both taken gravely ill, and did not recover, unlike the servants who had been similarly afflicted. Since the two ladies were heiresses, malicious stories began to circulate about the vicar. The official version was that the two had drunk water contaminated by the graves in the churchyard, and a new cemetery was opened, next to the main road. It seems that the stories were truly malicious; the vicar was a forthright and eccentric man who had upset local people, as had his black manservant with his pet monkey! As you leave the churchyard, you may also notice the **Bowdler** family gravestones, Mrs Bowdler being the mother of the editor of the 'cleaned-up' or Bowdlerized version of Shakespeare.

By the churchyard gate you will notice the first of our springs, and its existence may be one reason for the presence of the church on this site. To the north of the church is a house called **The Wilderness**, on the site of a mill, known as **Beckets** or **Bolloms mill**, its water supplied by this very spring. It is possible that this was the one owned by the monks. In the grounds of this house was discovered what was thought to be a large Roman villa, but the most recent excavations in the grounds of Box House, by Bath Archaeological Trust, indicate that the settlement was much more extensive than previously realised. It could simply be a Roman village, but it could be a religious site chosen because of the presence of the springs. The church itself lends credence to this theory, for the areas close to Roman temples were sometimes Christianized, Bath Abbey being the most notable local example.

Leave the churchyard by going back into its access lane, turn sharp L and go round to the R and downhill, when you will soon come to a small footbridge over the By Brook. (♦ This is where you will join the route if you did not visit the church.) Cross this and go almost straight ahead (perhaps slightly L) and upwards, keeping to the left of the wood. In 200m you will be on top of a short railway tunnel, and if you look to the right you will see, about 800m (½ mile) away, the first of our holes in the ground, the west entrance of Brunel's famous Box Tunnel. (You will have a closer view at the end of the walk, and so we will save our description of it until then.) Very shortly after this you come to a hedge and a gate. Do not go through this, but turn L, keeping the hedge on your right. Follow this hedge round as it veers R, always staying close to it.

(If you look to the left across the valley you will see the new cemetery, mentioned above, next to the A4.) *You cross a stile and then a gate, to come onto a track which leads to a lane at a junction. Turn L for 250m to another road junction. Here you turn sharp R and follow the slightly curvy drive towards a small group of houses.*

This little group of buildings was once all part of **Middlehill Spa**. The large house immediately in front of you is **Spa House**, thought to have been built in the early part of the 18th century. This is consistent with the fact that at that time the piece of land came into the hands of the West family, who were bakers. It was not until 1786 that **William West**, the then owner, decided to utilise the spring of mineral water on his property commercially, and turn the property into a spa. He added the rather plain house next door as a lodging house, and it appears the stables and outhouses were built at this time. Sadly the venture was not a success, and the creditors, who included the Bath architect **John Palmer**, had him declared bankrupt in 1790. He was allowed four years to pay his debts, but clearly abandoned the effort, for Palmer put the property up for auction in 1793, together with all the household furniture, linen and glass belonging to the West family. The bankruptcy document says that the family will be allowed to keep their clothes. The spa struggled on, and even in living memory there have been visitors hoping to take its waters, which the sale advertisement of 1793 described as "equal if not superior to the Cheltenham Spa". As late as 1876 it was described as having two springs, one "an aperient chalybeate, the other sulphurous, containing a large proportion of carbonic acid". Today it is a family home, and although the pump still exists, it is no longer in working order.

Go along the drive keeping Spa House (and most of the houses) on the left, but a couple of cottages on the right. You come to two stiles, the first a squeeze stile, leading into a field, which you cross. You should stay almost parallel to the hedge on the left, but gradually get closer to it, heading for a light-coloured cottage on the far side of the field. Cross into the lane and turn L to walk through the hamlet of Ditteridge (which is 1³/₄ km or just over a mile from Box, at GR 817694).

Ditteridge, though small, has a long history. It predates Box, and in Roman times may have been a hamlet on a route between the stone quarries and the Fosse Way to the north-west. The little church, which is up the lane on the right by the village cross (and kept open if you wish to make a detour), is the oldest in the group that now comprise the parish of Box. It dates back to Saxon times, with a mural of its patron saint, Christopher. **Cheney Court**, now a language school, is Elizabethan, and belonged, like Hazelbury, to the **Speke** family. The name derives from the owner of an earlier house, **Edmund Cheney**. During the Civil War, **Queen Henrietta Maria** stayed here for safety: it seems strange to think of this rather dignified lady, used to royal palaces, walking these same country lanes that you are walking today. The Spekes were Roman Catholic, although they observed the legal niceties by being buried at Box Church. Later the house came into the hands of the **Northey** family, who owned a great deal of the land in the Box area.

You should walk along this lane for about 500m. You pass a farm on the right and Cheney Court on the left. Then, after some open fields, you come to a small house, also on the left. In the hedge (which at the time of writing was quite tall), to the right of this house, there is a small gap with a public footpath sign (rather hidden) and a stile. Cross this stile, follow the hedge on your left for a little and continue on this line, which veers slightly L away from the lane. Do not go down to the left: you are making for the far left-hand corner of a piece of rough ground which occupies the right-hand corner of the field you have entered. [Note that the path is rather to the north (right) of the line shown on the OS maps.] After 200m you leave the field again by a stile and turn L down another lane; very soon the lane bears R and there is a track straight ahead which you take for 150m to cross a small stream and then bear up to the L to rejoin the lane opposite a cottage. (If it has been very wet recently, the track may appear to be a stream; in which case stay on the lane for 150m to a T-junction by Alcombe Manor, and turn sharp L to the cottage on your right.) Walk on a few metres to the next T-junction.

Opposite you there is a public footpath sign which should point across the field, taking an almost flat line. [The Right of Way follows this line, making for a point on the left-hand boundary of the field that is just before the far left-hand corner as you look at it; it then crosses that boundary and continues on the same line until it comes to a hedge going left, straight down the hill.] However, at the time of writing the farmer has left a clear path round the edge of the field, with a few waymarks, which we recommend that you use. For this, turn L on entering the field, then follow the border round to the R (do not go into the lower field at this stage). By a not very straight route, follow the left-hand edge of the field for about 350m to the corner. Here you should go down (L) into the lower field, but bear R to continue on the same line, now with the hedge on your right; turn L at the corner ahead and walk down the hill, crossing an awkward squeeze stile. After this you have to make rather an odd detour, because the Right of Way goes off to the left diagonally down towards the stream. So you bear L, go past the lone tree and almost to the swampy ground ahead; then turn sharp R and walk towards a gap in the hedge which is about 50m to the right of the brook. Here there is a double stile which you cross (it can be damp on the other side), and walk ahead, without gaining height, in a straight line for 500m, while the river (the By Brook again) veers away from you, and then returns. For the last few metres there will be trees on your left, and you come to a pair of stiles (at the left-hand end of the long and well-kept hedge) which you cross onto a lane.

The rather grand house that you have doubtless noticed up on your right is **Shockerwick House**. Pevsner attributes this to John Wood, but Tim Mowl and Brian Earnshaw, in their book about Wood, point out that as there exists a signed architectural drawing of this house by John Palmer, it must certainly be by him. It was the home of **Walter Wiltshire**, three times Mayor of Bath, and friend and benefactor of **Thomas Gainsborough**. He was a self-made man who rose from being a driver to run a carrier service to London. He refused payment from Gainsborough, saying it was an honour to carry his pictures. In return, Gainsborough painted his portrait. For many years the house contained four of his pictures including that of the actor **James Quin**, also a visitor to the house, as was **Henry Fielding**. Walter died in 1799, but the house remained in the family. **William Pitt the Younger** came in 1805, and here heard the crushing news that Bonaparte had won the battle of Austerlitz. Within a few weeks Pitt was dead, killed, it is commonly thought, by the shock of this defeat.

Shockerwick was, if not exactly a spa, the proud possessor of a holy well dedicated to St Anthony.

On the lane, turn L and immediately L again at a T-junction. In less than 200m you will come to the A4. (Here you are 4½ km or 2¾ miles from the start, and might have taken about 1¼ hours. The GR is 805681.) Immediately opposite you will see a footbridge which takes you over the railway; cross the road and the footbridge and continue up the track away from the line. (The fencing does not give you any choice!) You quickly come to another lane, where you turn R. After 100m, turn L up the drive leading to Sheylors Farm.

The lane you have just used so briefly was once the main road from Box, and the footpath exists because that was the lane to it from Shockerwick. The railway caused a rerouting of the road about 1840, to give access to **Box Halt.**

As you reach the farm you want to continue in the same direction, but keeping over to the R a little. Follow any signs there may be, which probably require you to keep R on reaching the farm, then immediately veer L and pass a small paddock (on your right). When you come to the large field, turn R for only a few metres and then L to cross this field at right angles. The line you want (which is a Right of Way) goes close by a power cable pole, heading upwards for the right edge of the small cottages ahead. On reaching these, join yet another lane, turn R for only 50m and veer L over a stile, to walk diagonally upwards (R) across a long field on the side of the hill. You should come to the top hedge shortly before you reach the corner; veer R to walk along with the hedge on your left to gain that corner, where there is a stile (though it may be rather hidden).

Cross the stile and veer very slightly R [note that currently the waymark, pointing left, is wrong; we think that the Right of Way may have been moved slightly] to continue along the upper boundary of the next field (with the hedge still on your left). You will almost immediately see a copse ahead, coming down into the field. Make for the first corner ahead on the left. Cross the stile, and go up the slope into the trees, using some steps straight ahead. At the top veer R and soon descend some more steps to another stile and back into the field. Ahead there are a stile and gateway; go through to rejoin the lane, which comes up from your right. Continue ahead past Springwell Cottage (on your right: the spring itself is low down on the left) to a T-junction, where you turn L, and after 200m turn sharp R along another lane to meet a busier road. Here you are 6 km or 3¾ miles, and 1¾ hours from the start, at GR 810670.

The slope you have just climbed is called **Wormcliffe**, whose name is supposed to derive from a legendary serpent which dwelt here. In doing so you have reached **Kingsdown**, over which came the original London to Bath road. In its heyday it must have been quite a bustling little community, and there are a surprising number of houses tucked away out of sight, including the old post office for the area.

At this point, especially if you are a bit late, you may care to know that there is a pub, The Swan, at Kingsdown, only a few steps away on your right. You could stop here for lunch instead of going on to Monkton Farleigh (which is just over half an hour further on). But you will, of course, have that much more to do in the afternoon. Although there is a final short cut to this walk, it will only save a quarter of an hour.

When you meet this road, cross it and turn L (uphill) to walk along it for only 100m, when there is a track on your right. You turn sharp R to take this track, soon bearing L and then R again. The track leads on past a small wood and comes to a gate and stile. You go over this, and the route becomes, briefly, less clear! Follow, for a few paces, the wall on your left; then when it turns left you bear L making straight for the left-hand edge of the wood about 100m ahead. On reaching this, follow on alongside it (staying in the field) to a stile. Cross this and, keeping to the same line, make now for the right-hand edge of the next wood ahead, going beneath some grid power lines. (As you reach the wood, you cross at right angles the course of a Roman road, though you cannot see any evidence of this now.) *Continue on the now clear track keeping the wood to the left, veering R at the end of the wood. In another 250m you come to a lane. Cross this and go ahead in the same direction for 400m (¼ mile), staying close to a hedge on your left, until you reach Monkton Farleigh at another lane. Turn R.*

Monkton Farleigh, as its name implies, belonged to a monastery, in this case a Cluniac Priory of the Benedictine order, dating from the 12th century. As we have already seen, especially if you have done the Pretty Villages walk (Walk 5), it owned or controlled considerable tracts of property in the area. Excavations have shown that the range of buildings here was quite extensive, but virtually nothing remains, except in little traces here and there around the village. Just before you emerge onto the lane in the village you may notice a bank on your right; if you go up to look at it, you will see that this used to enclose a large pond (now drained). This was the priory fish-pond; such ponds were not, of course, decorative, but provided a source of food. After reaching the lane, and turning left as instructed below, you will see in the field on the right a little stone structure, which similarly dates from that period, although it was reroofed about 1780. It is the **Monks' Conduit**, protecting the spring from which they derived their water supply. The spring was described as being particularly pure, which leaves one wondering about the normal water supply in the Middle Ages.

Beneath the same fields and slightly to the west extend man-made caverns, the result of subterranean quarrying for Bath stone, much of which comes from mines in the Box area. A tramway led down to a special halt on the Great Western Railway. During the Second World War, mines such as these were used as ammunition stores.

*After reaching the lane and turning R, very soon follow the lane round to the L and, after another 250m, turn sharp R at a T-junction. When you do this you will see the **King's Arms** just a few steps away on the left hand side of the road.*

The pub is believed by the owner to contain part of the monastery buildings; parts of it certainly date from at least the 16th century. If you look back at the pub when you leave, you will see that the porch has been added, and if you come out that way you may have to duck through the pointed arch of the inner doorway. That doorway is over 400 years old; the porch was an improvement made about 100 years later.

There was another spring here which supplied the pub and farm. The excess went into a cistern for the village pump, and from there was taken by earthenware pipes to a couple of turn-cocks in the village. As you walk along after lunch you may notice the evidence of this water supply. Several of the cottages are dated, including one (No. 82) which has a shell doorway. To the right of the village shop, there is a doorway with a pointed arch; this building was at one time the parish poor-house. As such, it was something of an incentive to avoid destitution. The church has been well and truly 'restored' in the late 19th century, leaving little of the earlier church to be admired.

On leaving the pub after lunch, turn R and go straight on, downhill; do not turn either left (back the way you came) or right (signposted to Bradford-on-Avon) shortly afterwards. Pass the church on your right and then, in a further 125m, turn L at a road junction (signed to Kingsdown). You walk along this road for 350m and then, shortly after passing a long line of trees on your right, you approach a house (also on the right). Immediately before this, turn R at a stile. In front of you is a very long, straight avenue, going gently downhill and with a line of trees on each side; behind you is the Manor House of Monkton Farleigh, which you may be interested to look at.

The **Manor House** is on the site of the main part of the priory, and has undergone several sets of rebuilding. The priory, a daughter church of that at Lewes in Sussex, was dedicated to Mary Magdalen, and her statue was reported to have a girdle wrapped and covered in silver, given by the empress Matilda. The patrons of the priory, the Bohun family, had come out in her support against Stephen. The priory's fortunes seem to have been somewhat variable, despite its wealth, for in 1472 the Prior of Lewes said there were not two monks of the order at Farleigh. Despite that, it was still in existence at the Dissolution of the Monasteries. The main church was destroyed by gunpowder, and the property went to the Seymour family, Dukes of Somerset. They disposed of it but in the 18th century it came back to them by marriage, and for about 60 years it was one of their family homes. The 10th duke refaced the 16th-century manor house, giving it a Georgian look. In the 19th century it was sold, and later owners made further alterations, leaving us with the pleasant if unremarkable house we see today. The avenue of trees appears on Dury and Andrew's map of 1771.

You walk down this avenue; for the first kilometre (over half a mile) the Right of Way is on the left side. When you reach the large wood on the left, you veer R to continue on the right side of the avenue to a stile at a cross fence. Go over this and continue straight ahead, taking care to stay on the line of the avenue and not bear right where there is also a Right of Way. This part of the avenue is also tree-lined, but only a few of these trees are still standing. At the end (and the whole avenue is over 2 km or 1¼ miles long; how imposing it must have been!) there are some old iron gates, with a stile just to the right of them. Cross this into a lane and go through a gate almost opposite,bearing L from the line of the avenue and following a footpath sign.

*This path crosses a field for a short distance and then takes an enclosed line past a shed on the left. You emerge in another, larger field. Your objective is the gate to the left of the farm complex ahead, and the Right of Way heads straight there, though it is sometimes easier to follow round the field boundary to the right. On reaching the gate, go through and make your way onto the lane. Turn R. You walk along this lane for 750m (nearly half a mile) but it is quite pleasant and you pass **South Wraxall Manor House** (3¼ km or 2 miles from lunch) on your left, along with a number of other interesting buildings.*

This manor house is perhaps one of the most interesting houses we shall pass today, being very little altered from its appearance in the 16th century when it was built for a member of the Long family, owners for most of its history. It is popularly associated with **Sir Walter Raleigh** who is said to have smoked tobacco here. **John Aubrey** certainly believed this, telling us that "in those days they had silver pipes. The ordinary sort made use of a walnut shell and a straw." Aubrey also narrates the story of the widow of **Sir Walter Long**. She had promised him that after his death she would not marry again. However, a man called Fox, "a beautiful young gentleman", persuaded her to break this promise. When they entered the parlour at South Wraxall after the wedding, the portrait of Sir Walter fell from its place, hit the bride on her shoulder and cracked. "This made her Ladyship reflect on her promise and drew some tears from her eyes." The family was rather prone to ghosts, for, in the shape of a pallid hand, Sir Walter's former wife had haunted the clerks drawing up a will on Sir Walter's behalf, in which he was depriving his son of his inheritance. It was one of the Long family who released the singer **Elizabeth Linley** from her arranged marriage with him, so that she could wed **Richard Sheridan**. It is said that this kindly man further helped from his own purse when they were in financial difficulties.

The gatehouse to South Wraxall Manor from a drawing of 1894

After the Manor House you pass Manor Farm, and you may notice that one of the buildings looks rather 'churchy'. This was the chapel of St Owen, held by the Priory at Monkton Farleigh. After the Dissolution of the Monasteries, it began to fall into disuse, until it became the farmhouse. It is now divided into about three dwellings.

At the end of this lane you come to a T-junction. Opposite, there is a gate *which you may have to climb over. A path continues ahead on the right-hand side of a hedge. Take this for 450m, veering L to stay close to the hedge, to reach a stile which you cross. (This is a squeeze stile with a top cross-bar which is hinged to ease your passage. Take note! One of us inadvertently came to grief by sitting on the top bar outside the hinge.) Turn L to continue, still with a hedge on your left. After only 60m a path crosses yours, and you should see a stile in the hedge. Do not cross this; instead, turn R here and go straight across the field to another stile. Cross this and veer slightly L and down to pick up a clear track in 125m. Bear R and go ahead towards the buildings of **Stonar School**, which is 5¼ km (3¼ miles) and 1½ hours from lunch, at GR 849656.*

Now always known as Stonar, after the school, the correct name of the building is Cottle's House, and the extensive grounds within which it once stood were called Cottle's Park. The first Cottle was Richard Cotel, who acquired the land in 1242. The present house, which can just be discerned among the confusion of school buildings, dates from the early 19th century, and is in the Gothick style.

Continue along the track, which becomes a drive, passing the school buildings on your right. At the far end, when the drive bends right, you go straight ahead and through the gateway, where you turn L. Go to the nearby field corner; you then have to cross a small field. It must be said that, though this is a Right of Way, at the time of writing the two boundaries are not very 'walker-friendly' and you may need to use some initiative to find the best places to cross! (For the first crossing, just to the right of the corner, there should be a barrier of barbed wire strands which, if you look carefully, can be unhooked to give access to the field - a 'pullover' gate. Go across or round this small field to an old gate which you should be able to negotiate without too much difficulty.)
When you leave the small field you should be in a larger one and close to a hedge on your left. (If you have the hedge on your right, a few metres along it you will find a gap and stile leading you through.) Proceed along the complete length of this field, to a corner at a small wood, keeping the hedge on your left. [However, you should be aware that the Right of Way goes diagonally R across the field, and then turns L to reach this corner.] At the corner you will find a stile on your left; go through this, turn R along the end of the small wood, and keep on this line towards the left edge of a much larger wood ahead. Before reaching this wood there is a gate; go through this and keep ahead (with the wood on your right) to the next corner.

At this point you cross the line of an old track. This is the course of the Roman road that we mentioned earlier, shortly before you reached Monkton Farleigh; this road, which you also cross on Walk 6, was the route from Bath to London, via Marlborough and Silchester. Here you can see the bank on one side of the old route: it is at least clear that the line was typically straight!

At the corner you continue ahead, doing a very slight 'R and L' through a small gate so that you are now walking along the left-hand edge of a long but narrow field (with woods close by, over on the right). Continue for 350m and you will see your exit gate ahead. The Right of Way goes straight for it, though a short detour round the edge may appeal. You emerge onto the A365 which, though narrow, is straight, fast and busy, so take care. Cross the road and a stile opposite, and continue away from the road near the right edge of the field. After a very short distance there is a stile on the R which takes you through into the next field. Turn L to walk with the wall on your left. Come to another stile to reach a lane, and turn L again; walk along the lane for 250m to rejoin the main road, bearing R along it for 60m, after which you turn R into a field with a wall on your right. (You will realise that you have made a slight detour; we have suggested this to avoid walking along the busy A365 for nearly half a kilometre.)

During the next bit of the walk you will pass the **Speke monument**, a reminder of a tragedy that some have turned into a mystery. **John Hanning Speke** was the discoverer of what he believed to be the source of the Nile, but **Sir Richard Burton**, explorer, translator of *The Arabian Nights*, and one-time collaborator with Speke, said he was wrong. There was a meeting of the British Association in Bath in September 1864, at which many explorers associated with Africa were to be present, including Livingstone and Burton. In this august company Speke was to defend his theories, knowing that Burton had prepared a paper stating his views. The paper was never read. Instead, the meeting received the shocking news that Speke was dead, killed in a shooting accident. In attempting to cross the wall where the monument now stands, he had put his gun down, which discharged, instantly killing him. Needless to say there were those who said that, unable to face Burton, he had committed suicide; but if so, it was an extremely convoluted way of doing it. It seems much more likely that it was simply a tragic accident.

Having turned R off the A365 you walk along the right-hand edge of two fields. (In the first, there is almost immediately a water trough on your right, with an attractive stone arch bridging it. And just before you cross into the second, the Speke monument is set into the wall, also on your right.) After the second field, cross the stile ahead (ignore the one on the right, where another footpath joins) and immediately bear L. You cross two fields diagonally, and then a paddock to come to a stile in a high hedge. Cross this.

*You have now reached the village of **Chapel Plaister**, which is 8 km (5 miles) and 2¼ hours from lunch. If you look half left, you will see a minor road opposite, leading off the main road (the B 3109) through the village; this is your onward route.*

Before continuing with the next part of the walk, take a small detour to the right to look at the building after which this little hamlet is named. You should quite easily find the simple chapel standing next to a cottage. If you are fortunate enough to find it open, go inside, for it is now usually kept locked. The first we hear of it is in 1340, when the Bishop of Salisbury granted a licence to the Rector of Hazelbury to preach in "the Chapel of Pleistede". Leland, writing in 1536, calls it a hermitage, but **John Aubrey**, describing it in the late 17th century, is almost certainly correct when he says it was "a place of entertainment for pilgrims that went to Glastonbury to St Joseph of Arimathea's Chapel". He notes the stoup for holy water on the outer wall, which can still be seen. An alteration in the 15th century gave it two floors, but with screens to the east so that the altar could be seen from either floor. This appears to have been to give separate accommodation for men and women pilgrims, while allowing all occupants to participate in Mass. The little room on the north side is thought to be the monk's cell.

Chapel Plaister in 1790 from a drawing by S.H.Grimm

By Aubrey's time, it was part of the neighbouring ale-house called *The Bell*, and later became a cottage. In the mid-18th century it became notorious for being the hideout of the highwayman, **John Poulter** or **Baxter**. Remember this was the main London to Bath road, and from here he had a clear view in each direction. Finally it was restored in 1898, though unfortunately the purpose of the two stories was not appreciated, and the 400-year-old floor was removed.

The next part of the walk takes you into the grounds of **Hazelbury Manor**, which has already been mentioned on this walk. There seems to have been a farmhouse here originally, which by Elizabethan times had grown into an impressive mansion. A survey of the 17th century shows it standing proudly in ornamental grounds. However, by the late 19th century that some very unhappy additions had clearly been made, to judge from Dr Tunstall's comment that it was "much disfigured by alterations, supposed to be necessary for modern comfort". Happily more thoughtful owners have since stripped these away and used archaeological and historical evidence to restore the manor to something approaching its original appearance. Although a large part is Tudor, part of what you will see today, such as the porch, is a clever 20th-century reconstruction. Behind the house is a field called Old Church field, and it was here that the local church once stood, and where those stone coffins were found that you saw in the churchyard at Box.

From the stile you bear left, cross the main road and take the lane ahead (coming from the chapel, this is a R turn), immediately turning R to go down the drive (which is clearly indicated) of Hazelbury Manor. This is obviously the tree-lined drive of a large private house: but it is also a Right of Way. Go forward, passing between high pillars and past some outbuildings on your left, almost to the gates of the house, and bear L along a track towards the shrubs. Do not then bear right (slightly upwards) which is private, or turn left (downhill) along a bridleway; instead, keep ahead on the level to a gate and a track leading across a field. This track is almost straight, but curves slightly R and equally slightly uphill. After 400m you come to a stile at a corner. Go over this and turn R to follow a path along the top of the escarpment with fine views over Box and beyond.

> *If you are late, instead of turning R you could go straight ahead down a track. (Do not turn L to another stile; you initially keep near a field on your right.) The track soon becomes a lane which leads straight down into Box. After 500m you approach what appears to be a T-junction (though it is a bit more complex than that), with a house called Townsend Cottage immediately in front of you.*

Cross the road to the house and bear L to go fairly steeply down a narrow but surfaced path. This is Glover's Lane; at the bottom, on your right, is the Chequers Inn where you pick up the main route description again at the point marked♦. This short cut will take about 35 minutes from the stile to the end of the walk, and save about a quarter of an hour.

The track is in fact the old route from the quarries at Chapel Plaister and Hazelbury to Box. At Townsend, Quarry Hill comes in from the right; this was the original route into Box before the London - Bath road was routed through the village. Hence Townsend really was the end (or start) of the town. Townsend Cottage was a little Dame School in the 19th century, and as such was rather looked down on by the official school in Box.

For the full walk, having turned R, continue along with excellent views for 400m to another path junction. Bear L here and go down into the woods, to follow a path below a small disused quarry and then, bearing R, staying quite level, passing an old building and a communications mast, both on the right. Shortly after this you will emerge onto a lane.

The quarries are the major reason for the existence of **Box**, which postdates Ditteridge and Hazelbury. **John Au**brey tells the legend of **St Aldhelm**, who threw down his glove while riding across Hazelbury and told the people to dig there, for they would find great treasure. So they did, in the form of Bath stone. The Bath Stone Company has his glove as its logo. Aldhelm was not exactly a disinterested observer; he needed building stone for his great abbey at Malmesbury, which is constructed of "Box ground" stone. However, there is strong evidence that the Romans were already working these beds. Originally most quarrying was on the surface as you see here, but the strata tilt at a greater angle than the hillside, so the precious stone had to be pursued underground. Strictly speaking it is incorrect to refer to stone 'mines'; to the quarrymen they were all quarries. Such a quarry is now open as a museum near Corsham, and is well worth visiting.

Turn L and after a few paces go over a stile on the R into a field sloping quite steeply downwards. Walk downhill towards the bottom right-hand corner (your line heads straight for the railway). Just before that corner take a stile on the R (there are two, and it does not matter which you use; but you should not use the gate higher up). Bear L and continue down to a gate leading onto the

A4, your line now being half R away from the railway. Turn L along the road for 100m when, on the left, there is a platform from which you get an excellent view of the west portal of Brunel's famous **Box Tunnel***.*

The tunnel was the most daunting obstacle to be overcome in the construction of the Great Western Railway to Bristol. Brunel, however, was not the man to be deterred by a little matter of a tunnel. The work took five years, during which time 247,000 tons of stone and fuller's earth had been removed from this $1^3/_4$-mile-long hole in the ground. The final cost worked out at £100 per yard, but there was a human cost too, for 100 men died in its construction. Some passengers were so terrified at the thought of going through it that an enterprising coach operator ran a service between Corsham and Box, allowing them to take what was perceived as a safer option. At the other end of the tunnel there was a subsidiary tunnel into the hillside, providing an outlet for the gravity-driven mineral line from the adjacent quarry. In fact, the quality of stone extracted during tunnelling work provoked a boom in the industry in this area.

From here, you could simply walk along the A4 through Box until, after about 600m (less than half a mile), you find the lane which leads down R to the Selwyn Hall and your car; but why not explore the bit of Box that is all too easily missed when you drive through. For the time being, cross to the pavement on the other side of the road, and turn L towards Box.

As you cross the railway, look to your right, where you will see the entrance to the short **Middlehill Tunnel**, on which you were standing at the start of the walk. These elegant tunnel entrances show Brunel's attention to detail. On your right, **Lorne House**, now a guest house, was once the home of the Rev Awdry, creator of "Thomas the Tank Engine", and shortly on your left you will see an engine in a front garden. It is not, however, a railway engine, but the sort of steam engine that provided the power for farm equipment. Called a Marshal Portable, it is now sadly lacking its interior parts and the fly-wheel which drove the attached machinery. In full working order, however is the old cheese press in the other half of the garden.

At the pedestrian crossing, cross the road again, turn R, cross Bulls Lane, and' take the hill sloping down to your L, marked as leading to Market Place.

On your right you will soon see the **Old Dairy**, indicated by the sign of a milk-churn. It continued as a dairy until 1968, and has an attractive rustic entrance. At the bottom of the slope you will see on your left the 17th-century *Chequers Inn*; most inns of this name derive their title not from a chequer-board but from the chequer or wild service tree, now quite rare (as is the word with this meaning!). This one is no exception. At the far end of the inn there is what appears to be a shop window, and the typical canopy with hanging space reveals it to have been a butcher's shop. It closed in 1959. The steep lane up to the left (which you will be relieved to hear is not your route) leads up to Hazelbury Hill and Quarry Hill, the old route from Chapel Plaister. This declined when the A4 took its present route in 1761. Called **Glover's Lane**, it is just one of many such lanes in Box.

From the Chequers, veer R back towards the A4. ♦ *If you have used the short cut and come down Glover's Lane, you continue almost straight ahead.*

On your right just after the Chequers Inn is **Coleridge House**. The poet **Samuel Taylor Coleridge** used to stay here, breaking his journey as he made his way to Nether Stowey. Then comes **Box Brewery**, now the home of an engineering firm. It was run by the **Pinchin** family, who had owned Box Mill for centuries. After it closed it became a badminton racquet factory. On your left you will see some very attractive 17th-century houses, and then, as you climb the slope, some cottages named **Steam Mill Cottages**. The steam mill to which they refer was a grist mill, producing flour. As you reach the top of the slope, and with it the A4 again, you cannot fail to notice on your right a very elaborate drinking fountain, in the high Victorian style. This supply of water was provided by **Mr Poynter** in 1894, on ground given by members of the Northey family. We have met them before as landowners; you may have noticed on your way into Box a pub called the *Northey Arms*. This is not, however, its original name. It dates from the time of the railway and was the *Railway Inn*. It is possible that the fountain is on the site of a spring, for Box itself had a small spa, though it only seems to have flourished about the 17th century.

Cross the lane to the fountain and look right along the A4. On the left you will just be able to see the school, which replaced the charity school. It was built in 1875, and has a miniature Big Ben. Pevsner is very disparaging about it, but others may feel it has a certain charm.

*Cross the main road to the **Manor House**.* This is early 17th-century, and was the family home of the Northeys. Next to it is **Manor Farm**, which is even earlier. It still has a fine barn, and the pound, where stray animals were kept until their owners paid a fine, has been converted into a little public garden.

Turn L and walk along past the **Queen's Head**. This is another ale-house that probably assumed more importance when the London to Bath road changed from passing over Kingsdown to its present route through Box. The Ionic doorway certainly dates from the 18th century, and appears to have been an attempt to make it look grander. Its stables are across the road, now used as the public toilets, although a tethering ring is still in the wall. The inn was also used as a courthouse, which probably explains the presence of the **Blind House** or **Lock-up**, just at the entrance to its car park.

You are now only 75m from the lane which leads down R to the car park. When you regain your car you will have walked 11¼ km (7 miles) since lunch. Our estimate of the afternoon time is 3¼ hours.

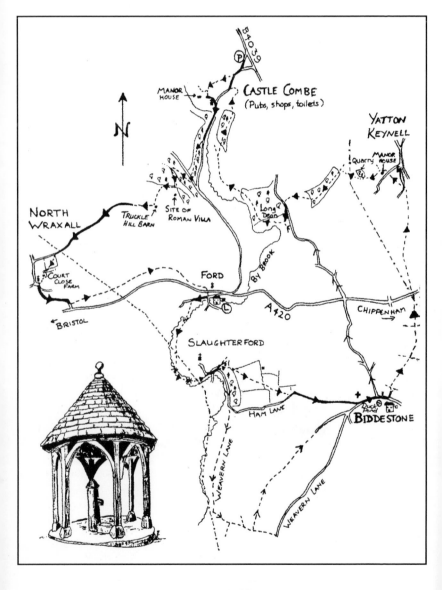

5   The Pretty Villages Walk

Location	West Wiltshire, about 22 km (14 miles) north-east of Bath, and 8 km (5 miles) west-north-west of Chippenham
Distance	7¹/₄ km (4¹/₂ miles) before lunch 11³/₄ km (7¹/₂ miles) after lunch
Time	2 hours before lunch 3¹/₂ hours after lunch
Maps	Landranger 173 (Swindon & Devizes) Pathfinder 1168 (Chippenham & Castle Combe)
Start	Main visitor car park, Castle Combe (GR 845777)
Lunch	*White Hart* at Ford (GR 841748) Tel: 01249 782213

This walk will take you through a number of North Wiltshire villages, during which you will discover that there is really no such thing as a 'typical' village: each has its own unique character, although individually many buildings within them are similar. The quality that they do share is that each in its own way has great charm. The best time to walk this is during the Spring, when it is still possible to glimpse views through the trees, but everything is just beginning to show green, and wild flowers are at their best. If you are lucky you may see, as we did, a new-born lamb, or deer disappearing into the woods. However, it is a pleasant walk at any time. During the walk, there will be frequent references to the 17th-century writer, naturalist and antiquarian, **John Aubrey**. Wiltshire was his home, and he went to school in **Yatton Keynell**. By 1691 he had written *A Natural History of Wiltshire*, a source of delightful though not always reliable facts about the area.

    Lunch: We have suggested the *White Hart* at Ford for lunch, but if you have made an early start, you may prefer to push on to Biddestone, 4 km or 2¹/₂ miles (perhaps 1¹/₄ hours) further, where the *White Horse* serves lunch until 2.00 p.m. This pub's telephone number is 01249 713305. If you are a visitor to the area, you may like to know that the *White Hart* (but not the *White Horse*) also offers accommodation.

    Note also that in very wet weather there are a couple of places which can become flooded. One is the stretch along the river just after leaving Ford; the other is Long Dean, near the end. If the first is passable, you will not have any problems with the second!

The starting point for this walk is the large, well-signposted visitor car park to the north-east of Castle Combe. If you approach from the north-west, using the B4039, the entrance to the car park is less than 100 metres down the minor road on the right. If you come through the village, go up the hill, bear left at the fork and the entrance is on your left. The car park can be busy, but you will not have any difficulty parking at the time of day that you will need to start in order to complete this walk. On a summer Sunday, in particular, Castle Combe and its surroundings are very popular, and you may find the last hour or so of this walk somewhat crowded.

Leave the car park and turn R (downhill) on the minor road. Bear R at the road junction and, 100m further on, bear R again off the road (there is a footpath sign to Nettleton Shrub), slightly uphill, and pass a school.

Sad to relate, the school is on the point of closing as this book is written, due to the creation of an area school at Yatton Keynell. The **Castle Combe District School** was founded in 1818, coming to this building in 1826. It originally had 34 pupils, but as time went on, it drew children from many of the surrounding areas which lacked facilities of their own. By 1846 there were 50 boys and 40 girls, though in severe weather the infants often found it impossible to reach the school.

Go between the stone pillars and, a few metres further on, over the stile on the L; then bear L and follow the path round the edge of the golf course which is on your right. (Watch out for low-flying golf balls!)

It was up on this hill, about 500m away on your right, that the castle was built in 1135 from which the village derives its name. It stood on the site of a Roman fort, which had also been occupied and developed by the Saxons. By the mid-14th century it was ruinous, and used by many of the villagers as a source of stone for their houses in the valley.

After 200m the path veers L and goes down through woods (alongside a wall on your left). Soon the path ahead bears right and levels out; but you must ignore this path and turn L over a stile (going downhill between walls, and under a small footbridge).

The grounds between which you are passing were once all those of the **Manor House**, now an hotel. It was originally built in the 14th century when the Lord of the Manor decided to leave the castle and come into the village. The house was virtually rebuilt in 1664 and has been

Castle Combe Manor House from A History of Castle Combe *by G. Poulett Scrope, MP (1852)*

substantially altered since, especially during the 19th century, at which time the gardens were landscaped. The last Lords of the Manor were the **Gorst** family, who finally sold the whole village in 1947. Shortly, you will be passing under the arch of **Archway Cottage**, one of two surviving gatehouses to the Manor.

Follow the drive and minor road, turning first L, then R, into the centre of Castle Combe (GR 842772) and stop by the Market Cross to have a look at the old buildings around you.

Castle Combe is perhaps one of the most photographed villages in the world, blessed (or blighted) by having won an award in 1962 deeming it to be "England's Prettiest Village". This led to it being used as the setting for the film *The Story of Dr Doolittle*, and as a result, being a honeypot for visitors from all over the world. It is hard to imagine it as an industrial centre, but that is what it was until the end of the 17th century, the industry being weaving. The man responsible for promoting the trade in the village was **Sir John Fastolf**, upon whom, so it is said, Shakespeare based Falstaff. He was certainly a shrewd man in many ways. He married into the **Scrope** family who had been Lords of the Manor since the reign of Richard II, or so Aubrey tells us. He then seems to have taken the running of the village into his own hands, and it was not until his death in 1469 that Stephen Scrope finally came into his inheritance. Needing plenty of cloth to supply his servants with his livery of red and white, Sir John proceeded to encourage the weaving trade in the village. It became a sort of free trade area, by which a clothman could pay a fee to Sir John, and then have almost free rein as to how he proceeded in business. By Sir John's death 50 extra houses had been built to accommodate the influx of weavers. Castle Combe was particularly famous for its ability to produce red cloth: cloth made elsewhere was sent there for dyeing and a check cloth in red and white, known as castlecomb, was made there.

The church, which you see to your right, is thought to have been founded in the 12th century, but was considerably extended during the 15th century, when the tower was added at Fastolf's expense. Today, this is the only really old bit of the building, for careless work by gravediggers caused the walls to show signs of collapse and meant the body of the church had to be extensively restored in 1850. If you have time, it is worth a visit, if only to see the clock which is said to be older than that of Salisbury Cathedral, made about 1380 by a local blacksmith.

The **Market Cross**, by which you are standing, probably dates from around the 14th century. It certainly existed by 1590, when the villagers were informed that they were to repair it. Aubrey tells us that Castle Combe had "the most celebrated faire in North Wiltshire for sheep" to which sheep-masters came from as far afield as Northamptonshire "but now", he says, "only some eggs and butter". There is a pump next to it, and a sign fixed on it by the local authority telling people not to deface it. The small stone construction beyond it is known as the **Butter Cross**, and is thought to mark the spot where there was a covered market hall, pulled down about 1840. Across the road is a timbered building, once the **Court House**, next door to which lived the constable. In your next stretch of walking look out on your right for **Reading Room Cottage**. In the 19th century, half of this was the **Manor House Laundry**, and the northern half was a reading-room set aside for the use of villagers. In another cottage there is a 16th-century nail-studded door, the only original such door left in the street. As you near the stream, you will see on your left the **Old Post Office**, a 15th-century house with the dormer windows added in the 17th century. It has been a shop for over 100 years. In the garden of the house opposite it is a medieval dovecote, not built as a pretty garden feature but as a source of food.

Leaving the Market Cross, pass the pump, bear R and walk on, gently downhill, to the stream and continue along the road.

The stream, which you will meet several times on this walk, is the **By Brook** which provided the necessary water for fulling and washing the cloth and power for the mills. When the flow of the By Brook declined in the 17th century, so Castle Combe's weaving industry declined with it. The houses bordering the stream here remind us of that prosperity, for they are weavers' cottages, with the house at the end being a master weaver's house. The wing is a 1960s' addition.

250m after crossing the stream you pass, on your left, firstly a bridge leading to a private house, and then a track over a footbridge. Continue along the road, and after another 125m bear R taking the footpath uphill into the woods. (This path is unmarked and not always easy to spot, so keep a good look out for it!)
Follow this path for about 500m to a minor road. On reaching this bear L and almost immediately turn R over a stile. Go into the woods and turn R immediately to take the clear track downhill for 350m to the valley bottom. It is often damp here! At the foot turn L through a gate and go uphill; you should be in the field, but at its right-hand edge, keeping close to the wood on your right. After nearly 300m (by which time you have woodland on your left

too) you come to a very rickety gate. Go through and turn R to follow the clear track along the edge of a field (initially with the wood still on your right).

Although there are no signs of it now, some Romans once had a home here on the edge of the escarpment, the remains of the villa being discovered in 1859. It was an oblong building, about 180 feet by 36 feet. The finds indicated a comfortable life rudely interrupted by turbulent events as Roman order disintegrated in the Dark Ages. Thought to have been a *villa rustica* used for hunting expeditions, because of the deer horns found, it was equipped with a suite of baths, with rooms brightly painted in red, blue and yellow. There were adjoining rooms for the servants, tessellated pavements, and a good water supply in the form of a well. But it is the well which gave the first indications of a violent end. The upper courses were destroyed and 25 feet down one human body was discovered, with, 15 feet below that, another two: the shaft also contained turned stone columns as well as rubbish. The bath floor appeared to have been roughly relaid after being broken, indicating some re-use after being partly destroyed. It is hard to imagine such events taking place here, in this peaceful field.

Keep along the boundary of this field, bearing L away from the wood to **Truckle Hill Barn** *(now converted to a house) which soon becomes clearly visible (2³/₄ km, 1³/₄ miles and 50 minutes from the start; GR 834759). On reaching Truckle Hill Barn go straight ahead through two gates, ignoring the driveway on the right. After going through the second gate, turn R immediately and follow the track keeping to the crest of the hill - do not descend to the left. On passing through a gate, the track becomes a minor road. The next stretch is probably the least interesting walking of the day, but this is amply compensated by the wide-ranging views to both sides.*

About 1½ km (1 mile) after leaving Truckle Hill Barn, and (perhaps more helpfully) only 100m after passing under the grid power lines, you should bear L into the corner of a field. There is a footpath sign, but you have to cross a low wall. Walk diagonally across the field to the opposite corner. Go through the gate and make your way R beside some low farm buildings; then follow a waymarked post L through another gate (which you may have to climb), and veer R and L again past the former farm (now converted into flats), keeping the main building on your right. Once past the building, turn R again along the drive and you will soon emerge on the road in North Wraxall (4³/₄ km, 3 miles and nearly 1½ hours from the start, at GR 818750). Bear L here and go downhill, ignoring (except as a detour) the cul-de-sac on the left.

(If you do not like the look of the field and farm complex, ignore the footpath sign at the low wall and keep on the minor road, turning L on meeting the road at a T-junction 300m further on, and L again at the next T-junction by the church. This will only add about five minutes to your walk.)

The sheds and cowhays through which you have come were those of **Court Close Farm**. You have now entered **North Wraxall**, pronounced 'racks-all' by the locals although the old spelling of Wrokeshale indicates that 'rocksall' would not be incorrect. About 1912 the then rector, **Rev F. Harrison**, wrote a survey of the village which provided information such as that in 1799 the parish was paid for the destruction of hedgehogs, but from 1817 vipers (adders) were the problem, 4d being paid for each body. The church is dedicated to **St James**, and is 13th-century but with an earlier porch. The various rebuildings and additions seem to have resulted in a wonderfully lop-sided church, at least internally. On the west-facing side of the chancel arch is a medieval 'doom' painting, with the figure of Christ represented as an eye within a sunburst. The 1887 OS map shows the yews which surround the church and also the Rectory Pound, where stray animals would have been impounded. One rector was **Michael Wyatt**, cousin of the architect **James Wyatt**. Building clearly ran in the family. He rebuilt the **Rectory** which was described in 1783 as being sizable with some papered rooms, an indication of wealth and sophistication as wallpaper was expensive (and hence fashionable).

If you have a couple of minutes to spare, make a small detour along the cul-de-sac on the left just as you reach the road in the village. The old Rectory is then on your left. A little further on you also pass, on the right, the 15th-century **Chantry Cottage** (though it no longer seems to bear this name), which has an octagonal finial at its gable end. There was a chantry at North Wraxall by the end of the 13th century, with a chaplain to say masses for the founder (Sir Geoffrey de Wrokeshale) and his family. Part of the priest's stipend came from the endowment of chantry lands, which may have included the ground on which the cottage stands. Further houses along this short cul-de-sac are also worth seeing; but you must then return to the road and turn L to continue the walk.

As you follow the road downhill through North Wraxall you pass the **old schoolroom** on the left. A description of 1858 calls this "a pretty little stone built teacher's house and a school room with flagged floor and desks along the wall, erected chiefly at the cost of the clergyman".

We are told that 20 children attended, "taught reading and sewing by a middle-aged mistress and writing and summing by the organist".

Continue downhill and then, passing **Court Cottage** *on your right, gently up. Soon there is a wood on your left, and then the road turns R. About 75m after the turn (and before you reach the main A420 road), turn L beside a bungalow along an Old Coach Road, now an unsurfaced and sometimes muddy lane, proceeding slightly north of east.*

This lane was once a main highway, principally to Bristol, but also allowing a route to Wales avoiding the city itself. Until the railway came, Harrison tells us, this was busy with all the traffic to and from America, the West Indies and Ireland. Teams of Irish reapers passed along it, as did livestock of all kinds. There were six pubs in four miles, for travellers are thirsty. The road was first turnpiked in 1727, but the gate was repeatedly destroyed, and despite clear evidence brought against the perpetrators, juries kept acquitting them, so unpopular were the tolls. Your route to the pub follows the line of the old road.

Stay on this lane, initially flat and then gently downhill, for 1³/₄ km (1 mile). You will then come to the edge of the village of Ford; keep straight on (bearing downhill if there is any doubt) until the lane emerges on a main road (the A420). **Cross the road with care***, and take the little footpath down some steps immediately opposite.*

This footpath is still on the line of the old road, which went past the pub and south-east up the hill, before rejoining the present road at Giddeahall. In 1752 improvements were necessary for, as one account says, "the road is in part so bad and even ruinous, that especially in the winter season, travellers cannot pass and repass without great danger".

In a very short distance the path brings you to another, minor road, when you will see the welcome sight of the White Hart straight in front of you (7¹/₄ km, 4¹/₂ miles and 2 hours from the start; GR 841748).

The **White Hart** reputedly dates back to 1553, and was a coaching inn on the road to Bristol. The stables have been converted into a house at the back. It also incorporates a mill whose barn and stables are the buildings across the road to your right.

After lunch in the White Hart, return to the minor road where the little footpath emerged (do not go down to the stream) and turn L. Walk along this road for 250m. **Take great care along here***; there is no pavement and the road is narrow, with high hedges and poor visibility for both traffic and walkers. Immediately after the last house on the right, turn L to cross a stile. Follow an indistinct track, keeping close to the stream on your left. After 70m you pass a plank bridge on the left, leading to private ground; ignore this. Some 250m from the road you reach a footbridge over the main stream, at a weir and under some trees. Cross this and bear R.*

For the next kilometre (³/₄ mile) you want to follow the By Brook downstream, but the first 600m of the route is not very clear on the ground. You could follow the stream closely; this is quite safe, but very lengthy because of its twists and turns, and you will have to divert inland once or twice to cross ditches. The correct course is to keep to the left-hand edge of the flat ground adjoining the stream, keeping a slope immediately on your left, and bearing gently L. If you start to climb, you have gone too far to the left. In the first 600m you should cross three fields, passing firstly over a stile at a gap in a hedge, then, in the second field, under those ubiquitous electricity cables (you will not see them again, you will be glad to learn) and through a clear gap in a hedge, right beside the river. On entering the third field you will see a rather ugly construction ahead of you. You should make for this; it proves to be a sluice gate. Cross the stream by this gate (there is no difficulty), turn L and **keep close to the stream** *(on your left) for 200m to a footbridge, which you cross. (If you veer away from the stream to the right, you will probably not see the bridge at all, thanks to the trees and the twists and turns of the water.) Follow the track straight ahead (but look out for the old mill-wheel on your left) for 200m from the footbridge to the road in the small village of* **Slaughterford** *(just over half an hour from Ford; GR 840738).*

The popular explanation for the name of the village is that there was great slaughter here in 879, when **King Alfred** defeated the Danes, but the most likely meaning is 'the ford by the black thorns'. There were cloth mills here, from the 16th till the 19th centuries, and it is possible that the water wheel you saw marks the site of one. However, by the time the wheel was installed it was a rag mill, making 'stuff', the raw material of paper-making. This industry has been carried on in this valley since the 17th century, and continues today.

If you have a moment to spare, just go up the lane to your left for less than 50m and look at the garden wall on your right. Along the stretch where it is at its highest you will see four most interesting 'roses' made out of stones and set into the wall. Now return to pick up the route of the walk.

Go straight ahead beside the stream for 75m and bear L at the junction (do not cross the bridge) along the road for another 100m. (The rather unglamorous remaining paper mill can be seen among trees on the far side of the stream.) *Here the road turns R. For the 'standard' route you should, at this corner, take the marked footpath that goes almost straight ahead steeply up into some woods (not the bridle path which is the track bearing off slightly to the left at a gentle slope.) (There is a longer option which is much to be recommended if you have the time and energy, but it is some 2½ km (1½ miles) and ¾ hour longer than the standard route. It is described starting at the paragraph marked ◆ below, and it rejoins the main route at Biddestone, the next village.)*

There are a few steps and then you will quickly come to a stile, and emerge from the wood at the foot of a steep field. Climb straight upwards on the steepest line, keeping woodland on your right hand, and always making for the nearest point of the line of low trees on the skyline. The climb is quite steep until you reach these trees, but also short; it should not take you more than 10 minutes or so, after which things ease off substantially. When you reach the trees you should reward yourself by stopping and looking back, as the view is rather fine.

In particular you should notice Slaughterford's church, set in splendid isolation in the middle of a field. It is comparatively modern, being built in 1823. Cromwell's soldiers destroyed the old one as they passed through on their way to Bristol and Ireland. By Aubrey's day it was a ruin: "the very barres are taken out of the windows". Instead the villagers had to go to Biddestone.

Go through this line of trees and bushes and bear R along the edge of the field for less than 100m to a stile. Cross this, and bear L to cross a field diagonally, moving away from the wood. As you come over the brow of the hill you will see a stile about 40m left of the far corner of the field. Make for this and continue in the same direction, passing close to the corner of a wall on your right and heading for yet more woodland (the right-hand edge of the main group of trees is the best line). As you get nearer the trees you will see ahead a stile, and footpath sign pointing back in the direction you have come from. Cross the stile onto a minor road (which is called Ham Lane), bearing L. You follow this road for about 1 km (½ mile) into Biddestone. In the village keep straight on, past the church on your left,

until you reach the main road through the village and see the attractive
green, with a pond on your right. (Just before you reach the pond there are
some public conveniences on the right.) Biddestone, which is 4 km, 2½
miles and 1¼ hours from Ford (at GR 863735), is an attractive spot, and you
may wish to spend a little while here.

Were anyone to select the perfect English village, with all the
elements that one imagines, then **Biddestone** would be in with a
very strong chance. It has a pretty little church, a very beautiful
manor house, and a village green complete with duck pond (and
ducks) surrounded by picturesque buildings, including two pubs.
You come to the church first; it is dedicated to **St Nicholas**, and
sports an unusual bell turret. The doorway clearly declares itself to
be Norman, as is the font. The gallery was probably erected during
the 18th century, and was intended for the villagers of Slaughterford.
Relations between the two villages were not good, with the result
that it was built so that it could not be entered from inside the church.
Thus the inhabitants of Biddestone did not have to mingle with their
unwanted companions. As soon as the Slaughterford church was
rebuilt, a new internal staircase was constructed at Biddestone.

The handily placed public toilets were constructed out of the
old **dog pound**, while on the other side of the road can be found
the **village pump**, protected by a cover, and just declared to be the
village logo. The **duck pond** was formed by channelling several
springs, and the locals firmly believe that their pond is the one
where one moonlit night some Excise officers disturbed smugglers
about to retrieve their contraband. When the Customs men asked
what they were doing, they replied that they were trying to catch
the cheese which they could see in the pond. From this, Wiltshire
folk derive their name of Moonrakers. However, this tale is also
claimed by Bishops Cannings, All Cannings, and Devizes. The first
of the two pubs, the *White Horse*, faces the green and on warm
summer evenings skittles is played outside. This pub is usually open
all day. The date of 1872 refers only to the porch. The main building
is at least 300 years old, and its foundation may well go back to
the 11th century. The monks at Monkton Farleigh (see Walk 4) had
a hostelry here which was a rest house for travellers and pilgrims.
Originally called *The George*, its name was changed because there
were so many George Inns. According to Aubrey, the beer brewed
there was diuretic. "I knew some that were troubled with the stone
and gravell goe often thither for that reason," he says. Another
spring in the village was famous for curing rickets.

You do not pass the **Manor House** on this route; it is on the eastern side of the village, and sometimes the gardens are open under the National Gardens Scheme. If the opportunity arises, these would be worth a visit. The house once belonged to the **Mountjoy** family, who continued to live in the area until quite recently. In its grounds stood the second of Biddestone's churches, **St Peter's**, pulled down in 1840. To make up for missing the Manor, you can see the beautiful early Georgian **Willow House** looking out across the green, with its cottage neighbours. Many of these have long windows, to give light for working at the looms, for this too was a woollen weaving village. When that trade failed, a blacksmith had a forge by the green to make agricultural equipment.

♦ *If you want to take the longer alternative mentioned above, turn R and follow the road uphill for a further 500m. The road then turns left, more steeply uphill: however, you continue straight ahead along Weavern Lane (keeping a couple of houses on your right). Weavern Lane has a tarmac surface to start with, but it soon degenerates into a track and after a short while it can be very damp and muddy. But this is the worst spot and it is worthwhile continuing! From the start of Weavern Lane you walk for about 1¼ km (¾ mile) with no navigational decisions to take. Perhaps this is just as well, as you may be concentrating on your footing! The lane then (at GR 841722) turns L up the hill, and you follow it for a further 550m from that corner. You will pass, firstly, a bridle path on the right; secondly, a footpath which goes sharply left back towards the woods; and thirdly, 120m later, another footpath going L over a stile. Naturally the first and second are clearly marked, but the third is more elusive and that is the one you want. (But if you should miss it just keep on Weavern Lane, turning L again shortly, which will also bring you into Biddestone.)*

After turning L and crossing the stile you go straight ahead along the edge of several fields, always keeping the hedge (or the remains of it) on your right; there is a small wood 100m to the right, and a farm to the left. Along here the views, especially to the south-west (left and somewhat behind you), are very fine. Your path eventually joins the road from the farm, on which you continue ahead to the village of Biddestone. Keep straight on, passing the church on the left, at which point you rejoin the main route. (If you take this longer alternative, then Biddestone is 6½ km, 4 miles and 2 hours from Ford.)

From Biddestone you have about another 2¼ hours to go. (If this seems too daunting, then there is a shorter route which rejoins the main walk at

Long Dean. It will save about 45 minutes, but involves about 2½ km of walking on roads. It is described below in the paragraph marked ♣.)

Bear slightly R and make for the far corner of the green in the middle of Biddestone, passing the White Horse and the War Memorial, and crossing the main road in the process. You should now be in the lane called **Harts Lane**. Follow this lane to the L alongside some houses on your left, and very soon bear L again following the Public Footpath sign (do not go ahead into Home Farm). You pass, on the left, the most inconspicuous sub-post-office we have ever seen, and then go over a stile, bear L and go diagonally across the small paddock to a squeeze stile. Go through this and veer R to head away from the village, and walk along the edge of the field keeping a hedge on your right.

At the end of this field there is a stile just to the left of the corner. Cross the farm track to another stile opposite. Bear R in this next field in order to walk, as nearly as you can estimate it, in exactly the same direction that you were following in the previous field. You should see two large gateways; make for the left-hand one, go through and veer slightly L. Pass close to a hedge corner on your right and keep straight on, following a (normally) fairly clear track, to the far right corner of this field. Shortly before the corner, there are two gates side by side on your right. Go through the left-hand of these gates and turn L, so that you continue in the same direction past a low barn, now with a large hedge on your left. (If it is very muddy you may need to detour to the right to avoid the worst parts.)

You next pass under some cables (this is a different set!) and come to a stile by a gate. Go over this, and take care in crossing the main road (the A420 again). Cross a stile on the other side. You now have to cross four fields on the way to Yatton Keynell (pronounced 'kennel'). In the first one the Right of Way goes straight across the field, parallel to the hedge, but you may prefer to walk along the left edge of the field, only 50m to your left. At the far side (and about 50m right of the corner) cross a stile, a ditch and a stone stile and proceed ahead in exactly the same direction, making for the corner which is at the left-hand end of a row of straggly trees, and becomes clearer as you get closer. Pass through a gap just right of the corner, and continue beside the hedge on your left; when this hedge turns sharp left, you keep straight on across the field, bearing slightly L to the corner. (You could follow the edge of the field if you prefer.) Just to the right of the corner you can cross over another ditch into the fourth of these fields, which you cross bearing R, aiming for the corner and the further gap in the wire fence on the right. Near the corner this gap leads into a car park (which serves the Yatton Keynell Village Hall). Here you are 7 km (4½ miles) and 2 hours from Ford (at GR 866761).

Go through and onto the minor road, and cross the awkward stone stile opposite. Walk straight across this grassy field, towards the isolated *house, and cross another stone stile onto another minor road. Turn R and almost immediately L.*

You will no doubt have noticed the attractive tower of Yatton Keynell's parish church, which is dedicated to **St Margaret of Antioch**. This unusual choice of patron saint came about when the church was rebuilt in 1230 by Sir William Keynall, after his successful return from the crusades. As mentioned at the start of this chapter, John Aubrey went to school in the village and tells how the rector used old manuscripts from Malmesbury Abbey to cover his books and act as bungs for his barrels of ale. "In my grandfather's dayes," remarks Aubrey rather charmingly, "the manuscripts flew about like butterflies." The name was originally Eaton Kaynel, and was sometimes referred to as Church Eaton. Unfortunately, the only part of the village which we have time to see on the walk is the house in front of you, **Yatton Keynell Manor House**. This attractive building dates from 1659.

Yatton Keynell Manor Farm from a drawing of 1894

Go through the gate on the right-hand side of the group of buildings, and follow the track. Keep close to the wall and buildings on your left, turning L past the entrance to the farmyard (but do not enter it) and another barn. You leave all the farm buildings on your left, with the exception of one very old barn which is so ivy-covered that you may hardly notice it. [At this point we must mention that the precise route of the Right of Way for the next 500m is currently under discussion. The line shown on the OS maps is unusable; it goes through an impenetrable and dangerous disused quarry. We describe the 'obvious' line, which is a 'permitted variation' and is preferred by the landowner, and mention an alternative should this line become blocked again, as it has been in the past.]

Cross a gate ahead (which at the time of writing is in very poor shape) and go downhill on a sunken track between walls. After 120m you come to another similarly dilapidated gate. Cross this into a field. Keep on downhill, with a wall not far away on your right; you soon find yourself in a pronounced valley and you should stay at its foot, where the path becomes ever clearer. After 150m there is a wire fence going across, with a stile (the quarry is to your right at this point). Cross the stile and pass below your last set of electricity cables, continuing downhill for 250m or so to a larger valley which goes across yours. In wet weather the ground at the junction of the valleys can hold a small pond, or at least be marshy, but in dry conditions there is no sign of this. Keep right of the marsh, potential or actual, and make for a gate leading L into the wood on the far side of this larger valley. Go through this: you are now in a Nature Reserve (and so, if you have a dog with you, make sure that it is on a lead).

[If the sunken track should be overgrown and impassable you could keep near to it, but in the field on its right. After 150m make your way down L to the wall and cross at a convenient point into the next field - take care, the ground is much lower on the other side! Turn R to resume the route just described.]

*Once in the Nature Reserve, you join a track and the route becomes much clearer. Follow the track to the other end of the wood. Go through another gate and take a small path bearing R and uphill for a few paces; then follow a path with scrub (and sometimes a stream) to your left and a wire fence to the right. After about 350m you should follow the stream (or its bed) round to the L, keeping fairly close, and in another 100m you will come to a hidden gate leading onto a minor road. Turn L onto this road and immediately take the small lane bearing off R. In another 200m, on reaching the foot of this lane by a few houses, turn R, noting the red **VR letter box** in the wall on your right as you do so. This hamlet is known as Long Dean, and is 9¼ km (5¾ miles) and 2¾ hours from Ford.*

♣ *For the shorter route from Biddestone, turn L at the pond and follow the road, keeping straight ahead at the junctions (at the first junction, where the main road bears right, you follow the sign to Slaughterford,* *not Giddeahall; at the second junction, where a road bears left, you follow the signs to Giddeahall and Ford, **not** Slaughterford). On reaching the Crown Inn at Giddeahall, go ahead to cross the main A420 road and continue straight ahead along the minor road opposite (signposted West Yatton). At the next minor junction, keep L; 200m further on, stay on the lane by veering R (left is a private drive). In another 500m you go down a fairly steep hill. 100m after the foot of this hill, turn very sharply L down the lane to Long Dean. When you enter this lane you rejoin the main route. This short cut will save you about 2½ km (1½ miles) or 45 minutes; however it involves walking on roads for about the same distance.*

You have returned to the By Brook, which runs in the valley below you. This particular stretch of the stream had a whole series of mills, most of which do not survive, or exist only as parts of other buildings. Some were for cloth and others for paper, like the one which Aubrey tells us was built in 1635 to make brown paper. It reputedly had a trough made out of a single great oak tree. That was somewhat downstream, but you will soon be passing (on your left) **Long Dean Mill** which still retains its water-wheel, although this is only visible from the other side of the brook. (If you look carefully as you pass you will be able to trace the route of the former mill-race which carried the water to the wheel.) Later you will see across the valley the picturesque collection of farm buildings where once stood **Colham Mill**. This may be the 'pretty villages' walk now, but in the 17th century it would have been a factories walk!

You now have a walk of about 2½ km (1½ miles) back to the start near Castle Combe, along a fine track well above the By Brook which you will see meandering around on your left. Initially the track climbs slowly; after two different, but excellent stiles it then becomes almost flat, and sometimes muddy. There are no paths branching off, but if ever there is any doubt stay on the level.

About 1¼ km (¾ mile) after the VR letter box you should encounter in some brambles a conspicuous post on the right hand side of the path. It is an old railway sleeper put to a different use as a signpost. Immediately after this, you want to bear R on a lesser path, going uphill to an old gateway after 175m, where there is a stile. (If you should miss this fork, it is not serious. In another 400m you will come to the road at the footbridge that was mentioned early on in the route description, and you can turn R and walk back up through the village to the car park.) Continue for ¾ km (½ mile), soon with a field on your right and wooded slopes falling away

*to the left. You pass through another 1½ gateways - at least, that is how
we counted them! - and then you come to a T-junction of tracks at a low
barrier. Turn L and go fairly steeply downhill, keeping to the main track
in the ditch; you will soon come to a road.*

The lane down which you have come was known as **Trim-tram** and
has brought you out at the top end of Castle Combe. On your way up
to the car park you should watch out for the remains of the **village
pound** and, firstly, the **museum**, built as a non-conformist chapel. The
adjoining cottage was once a blacksmith's. Also watch out for the
remains of a small surface quarry, at the fork in the road (on your left).
The large triangular area enclosed by three stretches of road (one the
road past the car park) is called **Bethel Place.**

*Turn R and walk up the hill. The road soon forks, and you bear L. The car
park, and the end of the walk, is then only 150m further on (11¾ km, 7½ miles
and 3½ hours from Ford by the standard route).*

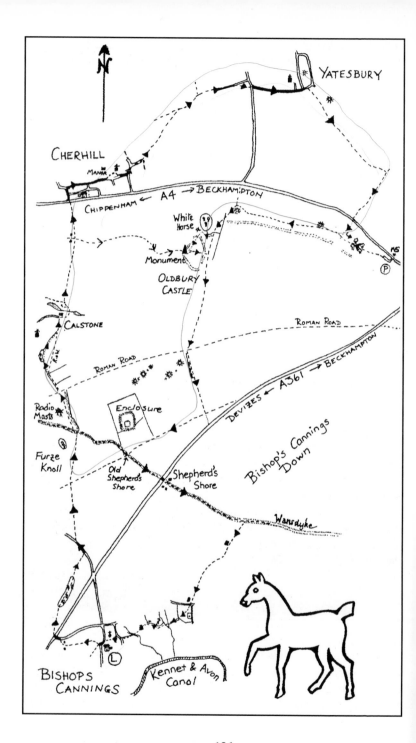

N

YATESBURY

CHERHILL

MANOR

CHIPPENHAM ← A4 → BECKHAMPTON

White Horse

Monument

OLDBURY CASTLE

CALSTONE

ROMAN ROAD

ROMAN ROAD

DEVIZES ← A361 → BECKHAMPTON

Enclosure

Radio Masts

Furze Knoll

Old Shepherds Shore

Shepherd's Shore

Bishop's Cannings Down

Wansdyke

BISHOPS CANNINGS

Kennet & Avon Canal

MS

P

6 Monuments, Ancient and Modern

Location   Between Calne, Avebury and Devizes, about 38 km (24 miles) east of Bath

Distance   11½ km (7¼ miles) before lunch
14½ km (9 miles) after lunch

Time   3¼ hours before lunch
4 hours after lunch

Maps   Landranger 173 (Swindon & Devizes)
Pathfinders 1185 (Devizes & Marlborough)
and 1169 (Marlborough Downs)

Start   Lay-by on the A4, 1 km (¾ mile) west of Beckhampton (GR 077692)

Lunch   *The Crown* at Bishops Cannings (GR 037641)
Tel: 01380 860218

This walk is a very fine one, almost entirely in open country with extensive views. There are a few ascents; none of them is steep but one or two continue for a while. Perhaps even more than other walks in this book, this is one to keep for a fine day with clear visibility. Certainly it is not recommended if the tops of the hills are in cloud or mist, as you will then need the OS maps, and good navigational skills, to avoid error.

It is longer than others in this book, but the going is nearly all easy, so you may well make rather better time than on the other walks. (However the timings we give are based on the same criteria as before.) There is a short cut towards the end which will save almost an hour.

The start point is a very large lay-by on the south side of the A4 road, 1 km west of Beckhampton (which is itself only 1½ km south-west of Avebury, well-known for its stone circles and other neolithic remains). From Bath it is easiest to follow the A4 through Box, Corsham, Chippenham and Calne, as other routes (e.g. using the M4), though faster, are substantially longer. If you miss the lay-by, go to the large roundabout at Beckhampton, where the A4 crosses the A361 Swindon-Devizes road, and then double back for the short distance to the lay-by, now on the left-hand side of the road. The entrance is opposite a milestone which marks 82 miles from London (as well as other distances too).

The word 'monument' has two principal meanings: the first refers to anything that preserves the memory of a person or event, and the second is any structure, natural or artificial that is an object of beauty or interest as a relic of the past. This walk contains an enormous variety of such objects covering one or both meanings.

The vast majority of them are barrows; those mysterious mounds erected some 5,000 years ago by the people who lived and worked here to commemorate their dead. The Archaeological Department of Wiltshire County Council produced a list of about 30 in the close vicinity of this walk, some of which are visible en route. We should not be surprised to find so many here, for the area was of religious significance. Not far away is **Avebury**, with its great circle of stones, and just down the road is **Silbury Hill**, which you may have glimpsed on your way here. Despite having reduced in height over the centuries, it remains the largest man-made mound in Europe, and its purpose is still unknown. However, we do know that barrows, or *tumuli*, are burial mounds, and they come in an assortment of shapes. The most common is the bowl barrow, a simple mound surrounded by a ditch, but there are also bell barrows which are usually for male interments, and disc and saucer barrows for the ladies.

The first man-made work to examine is modern by comparison. Before leaving the lay-by, look across the A4 to the milestone mentioned earlier. It is a reminder of days when travel was a far more daunting affair, for you are on the old London to Bristol road. Additions to the turnpike network then made it the route to Bath as well, but until the late 18th century the route then went over the shoulder of the hill, as you will soon discover.

As you enter the lay-by at the start (with your back to the roundabout) you may see on the skyline a monument, and this is your first objective, though your actual route initially aims somewhat to its right. It appears a fairly modest obelisk, not too far away; but appearances are deceptive! You are seeing only the upper part of a large monument, and it will take you some time to reach it. But do not be discouraged, for there is much of interest along the way. The monument itself will come into view, and disappear again, several times during your approach.

At the far (top) end of the lay-by there are a few trees, and a clear path through them which bears R and goes uphill to a larger stand of trees. Take this path and follow it through the stand of trees - and very fine beech trees they are too - continuing in the same direction for another 300m, with a bank on your right. At this point a track comes up from your left. Do not continue on the track straight ahead, but veer R for a few paces, through the gap in the bank, and then veer L to take another, parallel track in a grassy ditch with banks on either side. This track continues on the very crest of the ridge, and usually (except when the banks are high) you will have extensive views to both right and left. At one time, in the coaching days, this was part of the main road between London, Bath and Bristol!

The old Bath Road, which you will encounter later on, had become too hazardous by the mid-18th century, and this more northerly route became more popular, branching off the Bristol Road at Chippenham. The high banks were an attempt to shield the turnpike road from wind and weather. While you walk along its rather rutty surface reflect that it is probably in better condition now than it was in the 18th century.

As you follow the path, watch out for a large mound on your right, the first of the barrows (about ½ km from the trees). It is worth climbing to the top, but beware as you reach the lip; you will find it has been hollowed out. It was used as a defence post in the Second World War. From here, if you look eastwards along the road, you can see Silbury Hill, and there is another ancient feature to look out for as you descend back to the path. Some little way down the south-facing hillside, marked here and there by a line of rather scrubby trees, is a bank and ditch. About 2½ km long, and not always as plain as it is here, it is thought to be a boundary earthwork dating back some 3-4,000 years.

Continue along this track for about 1½ km (1 mile), at one point crossing what appears to be a small bomb crater (and probably is; there were several airfields in this area during World War II). Near the end, the track does a slight 'wiggle' to right and left around another barrow, and reaches a T-junction. Turn L, uphill; very soon some farm buildings come into view ahead. As you approach these, you will see a gate on your right just before them. Go through this gate and continue up the clear track to a second gate, where you enter National Trust land. Now there is a fence on your right; after only 60m or so, this fence turns R and you do the same to follow it uphill (leaving the main track). When it turns right again, bear R, making for the left-hand edge of the nearby clump of trees ahead. When you reach that point, you emerge dramatically at the top of a steep slope, with fine views to the west and north. The nearby village is **Cherhill** *(which you will visit later today); the larger town beyond is* **Calne** *and, still further away and less distinct, you can see* **Chippenham** *as well.*

All these views may, however, take second place in your attention. Immediately below you, on the steep slopes of the hillside, is the **Cherhill White Horse.** *It is, of course, not easy to get a good impression from above* *but if you wish (and not forgetting that you will have to climb back up again) you can go down the slope on the right of the Horse to get a better view. (Please do not venture close to, or onto the Horse itself, as these chalk carvings are very easily eroded.)*

This is not the oldest of Wiltshire's White Horses, but is probably the jauntiest. It was laid out in 1780, one **Dr Allsop** from Calne, known as the Mad Doctor, being the designer and promoter. He is reputed to have stood some distance away (the distance varies according to the authority one consults) and directed the cutting work on the hillside by shouting through a speaking trumpet. Even with such an aid, this seems ambitious; more probably he used flags. The eye was originally picked out by pushing the ends of wine-bottles into the chalk of the hillside, so that the horse literally had a twinkle in its eye. Unfortunately it did not take long for souvenir hunters to remove them. For those of you who like statistics, the horse is 129 feet long, 142 feet high, and the inner circle of the eye is 4 feet across.

At this point (i.e. the top of the slope) your route turns L towards the monument, which is now, at last, quite close. There is (at least initially) a clear track to it, though if after 50m you take the rather lower, less distinct one to its right, and look back from time to time, you will find other good viewpoints for the White Horse. On reaching the monument (which is 3½ km (2¼ miles) and an hour from the start, at GR 048693) you will no doubt wish to inspect it from all sides.

The obelisk, dating from 1845, is called the **Lansdowne Monument**, and was erected by the 3rd Marquess of that ilk. Although originally it had no inscription, it is known that it was built to commemorate one of his ancestors, **Sir William Petty**. Of him **Samuel Pepys** said that he was "one of the most rational men that ever I heard speak with a tongue". The designer of the monument was **Sir Charles Barry**, better known for his work at the Houses of Parliament. He was employed by Lord Lansdowne at **Bowood**, the family home at nearby Calne, where he was responsible for the clock tower and the main entrance gate. Unfortunately uneven settlement rendered the obelisk dangerous, but it has now been restored. Presumably it was during this work that it acquired the bolts which run up its sides: you may like to speculate on their purpose. We have our own ideas.

The next part of the walk takes you through **Oldbury Castle**, an Iron Age hill-fort. It was defended by a double set of 'walls' (the archaeological term is 'bi-vallate') except along the escarpment where a single line was sufficient. The entrance was to the east. However, it seems never to have been completed. On the eastern side the ramparts are unfinished, while to the west, part of the ditch remains undug. In the 19th century, digging for flints eroded much of the western part of the fort, but at the same time finds such as Roman coins were made. Later excavations have yielded domestic items such as loom weights and a weaving comb, suggesting that the fort was used as much for a settlement as for defence.

To continue, face that side of the monument which carries the commemorative plaque and turn L through 90°. Now take the track which bears L across the top of Oldbury Castle (and is only a little to the right of your line of approach to the monument). After 100m or so you will see a clear gap in the far ramparts: make for this gap and go through it. (Here you see the ramparts at their best.) *The track bears R for 50m and then turns sharp left. When it goes left, you turn R to walk across soft, short-cropped grass. Keep almost parallel to the fence about 75m away on your left, but if anything move gradually towards it. After 200m the ground ahead starts to fall away, and you should see a gate in a fence in front of you. [There is also a stile by the fence corner some 60m to your left. At the time of writing there was evidence of new fences being erected in this area, but the route we have described is a Right of Way on National Trust land and will remain open, even if a few details change!]*

Go through the gate and take the path leading downhill. There is another gate, and the path continues more gently downwards with a fence on your left, towards a line of trees ahead.

Just before you reach the trees you encounter a cross path (which you are not going to use.) This is a much earlier route between Bath and London, for it is the **Roman road**, which goes by way of **Silchester**. Here it is aiming for **Cunetio**, the Roman name for the village of Mildenhall near Marlborough.

When you reach the trees, veer L and walk along the edge of the field keeping the trees immediately on your right. After 400m the trees come to an end but you continue in the same direction, still with a wire fence on your right, for another 500m or so, until you come to a T-junction. This track across your path is not very obvious until you are nearly upon it, but don't worry, it is very distinct when you do get there! At this point you turn R. [Note: at the T-junction there is sometimes a track leading ahead, towards the main road about 150m away, but this is not a Right of Way and you should not use it.]

We are back to the age of coaching again, for this track is the **Old Bath Road**, which then continued over **Roundway Down**, where it can yet be traced very clearly, and milestones still exist. Try parts of it in wet weather and you will soon understand why travellers made their wills before setting out. From there it went via Sandy Lane down Bowden Hill to Lacock. If you have completed the Box walk (No. 4) you met this route at Chapel Plaister. Eventually, the difficulty and bleakness of the terrain, and the numerous highwaymen preying on its users, caused its decline. The highwaymen were particularly attracted to the steep hills, which slowed the coaches for them.

Having turned R you follow this new track, very gently uphill, for 1¼ km (³/₄ mile). During this stretch there are a number of things of interest to observe.

Firstly, on your right you may notice four conspicuous *tumuli*. In fact a close inspection of the surrounding fields will reveal that they are fairly peppered with *tumuli*, all round barrows of varying types. (Long barrows are more unusual.) Sadly, many are now disappearing, obliterated by ploughing. For some reason, there are several groups or clumps of them just here. (Your lunch-time occupation might be to think of a collective name for barrows!)

As you walk along you will see ahead on the right (below the large clump of trees), and also to the left (on the other side of the main road), a prominent line of ridge and ditch. This is the **Wansdyke**, and you will soon be walking along it for 2 km (1¼ miles) or so.

This is perhaps the most impressive stretch of this rather enigmatic earthwork, which some have suggested once ran from Portishead to Inkpen Beacon, although if so, it has disappeared in places. Its purpose is unknown, but it is now thought to be military in origin, rather like Offa's Dyke, and is probably late Roman or early Saxon. Needless to say, many legends attach to it, especially its name. One old name is the Devil's Ditch, built by him on a Wednesday. Others say the Saxons named it after their chief god Woden. There are other local names besides the Wansdyke which seem to refer to Woden, so it may be that the area was home to a cult dedicated to him. The date of the Wansdyke was in the past rather controversial, and **William Stukeley**, the 18th-century antiquarian, in his illustration of 1724 (on page 118), says triumphantly that it pre-dates the Roman road, because the latter appears to 'flow' out from it, but it is now thought that the dyke's builders used the Roman road, and particularly its *agger* or defensive mound, in its construction.

The view from Roundway Hill drawn by William Stukeley on 18th July 1723

113

Nearer the end (and also on the right) you may see part of an almost square 'enclosure' marked as such on the OS maps. (Do not worry if you miss this, as you will have a better view of it after lunch.) This is considered to be a **medieval sheep pen**. There is a smaller rectangle within it, thought to be the shepherd's shelter, although once again it has almost disappeared thanks to ploughing. However, photographs survive which show it quite clearly, and Stukeley indicates it very plainly in his illustration. Some pieces of green and yellow glazed medieval pottery were found within the inner rectangle, and are now in Devizes Museum.

After 800m (½ mile) or so on the track you pass, on the left, the drive leading to a nearby farm and, about 350m further on, you turn L at a small stile and walk along the Wansdyke, initially downhill. The path is not too distinct, but you want to stay on top of the bank all the time. Go down to the road (the A361), cross with care, and continue ahead just to the left of the farm buildings. For a few metres it seems as if you are walking up the drive to a private house but halfway along you will see a grassy track bearing R and going up to a stile. Once across this, the Wansdyke path again sticks to the top of the bank, and is much clearer than before. (You cross the A361 at GR 045662, about 7½ km, 4¾ miles and 2¼ hours from the start.)

The A361 was the **Devizes Turnpike Road** and the milestones have metal plates, some of which survive. This crossing point is called **Shepherds' Shore**. One explanation of this name is that 'shore' is a corruption of 'shard', a gap or break in the down, here created by the ditch of the Wansdyke.

From the road you need to walk for about 1¼ km (¾ mile) along the Wansdyke (crossing a few stiles which we do not mention individually) before you leave it. About half-way along, a track crosses your path. At this point you are still going uphill, and you must continue along the dyke.

We were told by a local resident that the hill on your left, called **Bishops Cannings Down**, was a dummy airfield during the Second World War. An inquiry to the RAF Museum about such airfields elicited the information that this could well be correct; there were at least two of these in the area. These dummy airfields usually had lights laid out in the pattern of a nearby genuine field, but in some cases actually had fake buildings and even dummy planes. They were spectacularly successful. Not only did they attract bombs away from the right target, but the German pilots, knowing of their existence, sometimes failed to drop bombs on the real target, believing it to be a replica. Eventually the Germans decided to rush through a similar scheme, but it was too late: efficient reconnaissance had already established the position of their true airfields. The RAF itself is not sure of the exact location of these fake fields, so there is scope for research.

*Shortly after this, you come over the brow of the hill and start gently downwards. Just before the foot of this slope, a second track crosses. On the left, it turns to run parallel with the dyke. To the right it heads towards a large black barn which you may notice as you approach (although it is not actually visible when you reach the track itself). You must turn R here (at GR 057658), and follow this second track past the barn. Soon after this you come to the southern edge of the downland, and a beautiful and extensive view over the **Vale of Pewsey** and beyond opens up. Nearer at hand, below and slightly to your right, you may spot a church steeple. This will doubtless be a welcome sight once we have added that your lunchtime pub is situated almost in the shadow of the church.*

Follow this track down until, about a kilometre (³/₄ mile) after the barn, you come past some buildings and reach a minor road at a corner. Almost opposite you (very slightly to the R) there is a public footpath sign pointing diagonally R across a field, and directing you to Bourton and Bishops Cannings. Follow this indistinct path, past the electricity supply pole in the middle of the field, to a small stile in the far corner. (If in doubt, keep just left of the left-hand of the two possible poles, making for the left-hand end of a line of low trees.) Cross the stile, veer R and walk along the edge of the next field with the line of low trees on your left. Cross a number of stiles and two plank bridges, and emerge into another, larger field. [At this point, if you have an OS map with you, note that the Right of Way has been diverted from the route which may be shown on the map.]

Turn R and then follow the field boundary, first to the L, then veering R and steering a wavy course, always keeping the boundary on your right. You pass (and ignore) a gate and then, about 250m or so after you entered this field, you will reach a stile on your right. Do not cross this, but instead bear L (aiming to the left of the church) to follow an obvious grassy path which now crosses the field towards the village. At the far end, cross a wooden bridge and bear R over the stile. Follow the path along the right edge of the field to another stile on your right. Cross this into a lane, and go L to continue in the direction of your approach, crossing another lane and walking along Church Walk. Not surprisingly you are always heading for Bishops Cannings church, for your way lies through the churchyard.

You cannot have failed to notice the most striking feature of **Bishops Cannings** church, its spire. At 135 feet high, it is an echo of that at

Salisbury. The old name for the village was **Cannings Episcopi**, and it was given by the Bishop of Salisbury to the Dean and Chapter in the 11th century. It also shares with the cathedral its dedication, which is to **St Mary the Virgin**. This spire was added in the 15th century, together with the stair turret, the little pinnacle next to it. This has given rise to a local story that the villagers would have liked two spires, so they manured the little turret, in the hope that it would grow.

The church is large, and has examples of several kinds of church architecture: Norman, Early English, Perpendicular, not forgetting Gothic Revival. Here we should not turn up our noses at the Victorian work, for it includes some fine carved pew ends by **Harry Hems**, added in 1883/4. This takes us inside the church where there is much of interest to see, including an unusual 'carrell' or box-like pew, decorated with some curious paintings. Its purpose is unknown, although it is sometimes called a confessional chair. The church organ is also notable, dating as it does from the early 19th century. It was given by a local man, **William Bayly**, who had been assistant astronomer to Captain Cook. The previous organ was given about 1593 by the organist Mr Ferebe, who seems to have been a very lively person. John Aubrey, writing in the late 17th century, tells us that **Mr Ferebe**, "an excellent musician", had trained his choir of parishioners to sing "the Psalmes in consort to the organ". When James I was staying locally, Ferebe entertained the King with "bucoliques of his own making and composing, of four parts, which were sung by his parishioners, who wore frocks and whippes like carters". After this interlude there was a football match, also arranged by the organist.

The church, in which there is an excellent guide book on sale, richly deserves a visit. Even if you decide not to go in, stop to admire the delightful picture created by the church and churchyard together.

*Go through the churchyard towards a thatched cottage, turn L on the road, and the **Crown Inn** is immediately in front of you on the left side of the road. Here you are 11½ km, 7¼ miles and 3¼ hours from the start (at GR 037641). You will find that the lunches are more than large enough to satisfy even the appetite that you have built up on your walk so far.*

After lunch you turn L along the road and immediately sharp R up a short drive which is called The Estate Yard. (Note: do not cross the stile that is actually on the road at this corner, with a Public Footpath signed diagonally across a field.) After 50m you come to a gate and stile. After crossing this stile, follow the path in the field, keeping close to the fence on your left and watching (after about 150m) for another stile in that fence, by an old tree. (If you reach a fence and gate in front of you, you have gone just too far and should go back about 15m to find the correct stile.) Cross this stile, and go R to continue in the same direction with the fence now on your right. After a further 300m you come to a farm, called West End Farm. Cross the stile and go straight ahead, between two small silos, continuing until you reach the last set of farm buildings. Turn R before these and go ahead to the minor road. The farm itself is usually full of pigs, and the nearby fields swarming with genuinely free-range hens. [Occasionally the 'correct' route through the buildings may be blocked by farm operations, but by knowing that, on entering the farm at the stile, you are making for its far right-hand corner, you should have no difficulty in making your way to the road.]

On reaching the minor road, turn L and walk the short distance to the main A361, which you meet at one end of a stretch of dual carriageway. As a result, the traffic is very fast, so take care as you cross. On the other side turn R and take the clear track which veers L and uphill away from the road towards a small wood about 400m away. On reaching the trees, follow the track L but only for 20m or so; then turn R through a new metal gate to take a path up inside the woods. The gate is of an unusual design, which we describe in the next paragraph. [There is a somewhat unfriendly notice beside it, but do not be put off: it is the farm track to the left that is not a Right of Way. To confuse things still more, the OS maps show the Right of Way on the eastern (right-hand) edge of the trees, but the path has been diverted and you should follow the footpath signposts, and our description, through the trees.] After going through the trees (they are in a fairly narrow strip) for 400m you emerge and turn L to follow a clear track for a further 400m over the brow of the hill and down to a road. As you come over the brow, you will see ahead a large circular clump of trees on the horizon, with two radio masts behind them; you will be making for these for the next half-hour or so.

Although the road is minor it is quite busy and fast, so once again you need to take care. Cross the road and turn L, walking along it fortunately for only 150m to the farm ahead; here you thankfully bear R along a signposted track, keeping cottages on your left and the main farm buildings on the right. By the time you reach the skyline you will have passed through five more of the new metal gates with their rather unusual design; there are two distinct ways of opening them. The vertical handle is, in fact, designed to be used from horseback and it is no surprise to learn that this part of the walk is on a bridle path. This does not concern you, as a walker, but we do advise you to count the gates! The first one, about 800m (½ mile) from the road, is where you meet a track (the Old Bath Road again) going across yours; the tracks form a T-junction but your path goes straight ahead through the gate. Continue to the second gate, a few metres right of the field corner. Here you need to continue upwards, but

Morgan's Hill and the Wansdyke drawn by William Stukeley on 20th May 1724 note that you do not go towards the metalled track that goes past the clump of trees, which is called Furze Knoll. Instead, keep very slightly R of straight ahead and go up in a slight dip to the third gate. Go through this, bear L and upwards to the fourth gate, which is only 50m or so from the third [once again we mention that here the Right of Way has been moved slightly from the route shown on the OS maps].

After you have gone through the fourth gate, you want to bear R and go just east of north across the field for 300m. But there is no sign of a path here, so (unless you have a compass) you need to aim to the right of the two radio masts, which are now quite close. (To be even more accurate, imagine that there are six masts, equally spaced, but that you can only see the two leftmost ones. Your correct aim is the point where the right-hand mast would then be.) Shortly you will reach level ground, and then descend slightly; at this point you should see the fifth and last of these metal gates in the fence ahead. Make for it, pass through and you will find that you are once more on the Wansdyke, now at GR 032669 (3½ km; 2¼ miles and just over an hour from Bishops Cannings).

This is a fairly high point of this ancient track, known as **Morgan's Hill,** about 250m (over 800 feet) above sea level. In the field below you, sharp right, is the enclosure that we mentioned earlier (just before you first met the Wansdyke).

Stukeley's illustration shows a gibbet somewhere about here, actually perched on the bank of the Wansdyke; according to one legend, the hill derives its name from a felon hanged here. As Katharine Jordan points out in her book about the folklore of Wiltshire, the presence of the gibbet is a strange coincidence, for Woden, legendary builder of the dyke, was god of the dead, and sacrifices to him were hanged. Today, instead of the gibbet, you have been observing the radio masts. This must have been quite an early radio station for it was certainly in existence by 1926. At this point the Wansdyke has tangled itself with an earlier earthwork, similar to the one you saw near the start.

From the last metal gate, bear L and go down into the Wansdyke ditch, walking along this (uphill) for just a few metres before turning sharp R along the edge of a field (actually, the field containing the masts). You do not cross any fences, but you should now have a wire fence (initially new, but soon quite old) on your right. Follow this field boundary round to the L (still not crossing the fence) and over the brow of the hill, when once again a superb view opens up, this time to the north and west. Continue, now downhill, for a short distance to a gate, where you enter Morgan's Hill Nature Reserve; then go more steeply downhill, veering slightly L away from the fence down a grassy slope, to a second gate leading onto a track (the Roman road again) crossing your route.

Stukeley's drawing of 1724 (on page 118) shows the Roman road and the Wansdyke, as well as Oldbury Castle. To the extreme left of the picture you can see your next objective, **Calstone**, a settlement dating from medieval times. You will be leaving the church well to your left and passing through the woods that Stukeley depicts beyond it. Above all, this picture shows how little these downs have changed in 270 years; the only difference is the substitution of the masts for the gibbet.

There is a footpath and Right of Way continuing ahead, down the hillside, and this is your route, although it is not as much used as the paths you have been on previously. To start, you go past an old gate or across a rather narrow stile, and follow an indistinct track. You should make sure that the tall hedge is on your left, and try to keep as close to it as possible. You cross a couple of old gateways, and come into a larger field; continue down beside the hedge. At the bottom turn R to a new gate which is just a few metres to the right of your natural line. Go through this, turn L and keep on down, keeping close to a small woodland on the left but not entering it, then curving R, still alongside the hedge. [Note that the OS maps may show the Right of Way as taking a more direct line across the fields to the right, but you are advised to follow the route as described. There are usually several electric fences around here, but we have always found adequate arrangements for walkers along this line.]

On reaching the more level ground at the foot of the field, the hedge turns L. Follow the hedge for 150m to a stile and gate, and a road end at South Farm. Here turn R and walk for another 150m, with the farm buildings on your left [you are on a Right of Way, as the large "Private Road" sign rather grudgingly acknowledges]. After the buildings, you see the new farmhouse, also on the left. By the wall, your track divides. You must take the left-hand track which goes downhill, curving L as it does so. It crosses a wooded valley, with small lakes to left and right (but these may not be visible through the undergrowth; indeed the briefly enclosed terrain is a real contrast to all that has gone before), and curves L again up into the trees. Just after crossing the stream, be careful to take the upper, waymarked track and not the left-hand one which is a private drive. In another 100m you emerge onto a wider track at a corner. Bear R and follow this track, slightly uphill and away from the woods (do not follow the edge of the trees, and do not turn right at the next junction, 75m further on).

There is now a fairly easy 1¼ km (¾ mile) to the A4 at Cherhill (pronounced 'Cheryl'). Continue straight ahead. After 800m (½ mile) you come to a couple of barns; you go straight ahead at this point, which is 6½ km, 4 miles and 1¾ hours from Bishops Cannings (at GR 032695).

From these barns the full route is a further 8 km (5 miles), and might take about 2¼ hours. If you want a shorter walk, you can turn R here and follow an obvious track back to the Lansdowne Monument which is about 1½ km (1 mile) ahead, from where you can retrace the outward route back to your car. This shorter route saves 3 km (2¼ miles) and nearly an hour. In view of the length of the full walk we describe this short cut in more detail at the end of the chapter.

*For the full route, continue downhill on a clearer track, between hedges, to the A4, a road which is sometimes busy but usually, in this part of Wiltshire, gives a pleasant drive. Just imagine what it would be like if the M4 did not exist! Sixty years ago it was far less wide: indeed this was reputed to be the narrowest and most dangerous stretch of the road between London and Bath. Cross and go ahead down **Oliver's Hill** for 175m, turning R when you reach the T-junction at the bottom into a road called, rather grandly, **The Street**. This narrow lane contains most of the older houses in **Cherhill**, and you will find plenty of interest here.*

The name of the village appears in Domesday Book as Cheurel, and the suffix '-el' is thought to mean 'hill', of which there are quite a number in the area. By the 18th century, there were several coaching inns locally, to provide a service for those travelling to Bath and Bristol. One of the best known was the *Labour in Vain*; it was on the main road but the name survives now only as the name of the hill you descended on the way to the A4, though it is not named on the maps. To travellers, Cherhill became notorious for the **Cherhill Gang**, a band of footpads (one can hardly dignify them with the name of highwaymen). Though many writers assign them to the 18th century, they must have been active early in the 19th, for some of them were alive (albeit as old men) in the 1860s. By this time, white-haired and bearded, these venerable ex-robbers appeared to be pillars of the local community. However, one of them recounted how he had been accustomed to sally out naked, with the result that victims were distracted for, one imagines, a variety of reasons. Thus they did not recognise him later. It should be said that throughout the coaching era, the whole of Wiltshire was notorious for highwaymen, its lonely downlands and steep hills giving these 'gentlemen of the road' ample scope to pursue their activities.

There is a pub in Cherhill, the ***Black Horse***, which is worth a visit. It will probably be closed at the time you come through: but perhaps a brief stop on your way home is called for? It is on the A4. (If you want to find it now, about 400m after entering The Street, turn R up a lane opposite 'The Orchard', then continue along a footpath to the pub.)

After 600m or so you pass a cul-de-sac on your left called Mill Lane, and shortly after this there is a drive bearing L through some iron gates. These are clearly marked "The Manor House. Footpath to Church only". Take this drive; at the top, go through the wooden gate (ahead of you, rather to the left) into the churchyard.

The church is worth a visit, and in walking up to it, glance at the **Manor House**. This is now rather plain and unremarkable, but parts of it are older than at first appear, particularly the wing nearest the church. It is possible that it was once a typical E-shaped Tudor house which has lost some of its wings, for there is evidence of their foundations. Some unsympathetic changes in the 19th century left it looking very plain, but its lovely setting has done much to restore some charm.

As you pass through the gate into the churchyard you are walking on the site of a Roman building, possibly a villa. Two pieces of a mosaic pavement have been found here, parts of which are now on display in Devizes Museum.

The church itself, dedicated to **St James**, goes back to the 12th or 13th century, the tower being added in the 15th. You will almost certainly have noticed that the tower is somewhat lop-sided. It was built on a foundation of sarsen stones, the very hard sandstones popular with prehistoric builders; both Stonehenge and nearby Avebury are constructed with them. As the first stage of the tower was added, the stones sank unevenly. Despite this, the second stage was added, causing further subsidence. Finally, in a bold if not foolhardy move, the builders added the third stage, but by this time the stones had settled into their final position, and no further movement occurred. The top now overhangs the base by 22 inches.

The church was once rather overshadowed by the tithe barn, the last wooden one in the county. Capped with a stone-tiled roof, it was 111 feet long with two porches on each side. These matching porches are characteristic of most tithe barns. At harvest-time the doors on each side were opened, and the grain was winnowed on the floor between them. The chaff was then blown away by the draught passing through the open doors. It was first built in the 15th century, but over the years the weight of the roof began to force the building out of shape, and by 1938 it was leaning somewhat to the west. Efforts were made to save the barn, but by 1956 the cost of repair was estimated at £12,000. Despite earlier rumours that an American was going to dismantle it and take it back to the States, no purchaser or well-wisher came forward to rescue it, and it was demolished.

On emerging from the church go ahead (this will be a R turn if you did not divert into the church) and through the main lych-gate back into The Street, turning L to continue your walk. Soon you reach a T-junction (Park Lane). Turn L. Ignore the first turning right (into Upper Farm) and, after 100m at the foot of the hill, turn R along a signposted By-way. After 175m, where the main track turns right, make sure that you bear L and keep going uphill.

While researching this book, it became apparent by talking to some local children that the villagers are proud of their home and its history. This is due largely to the efforts of a local historian called **Denis Blackford**, who in 1941 published *The Manor and Village of Cherhill*, an extensive and readable account of the area from early times. It seems to have inspired everyone to keep oral tradition alive, and as a result, one little girl had an explanation of the name of the lane along which you are now walking. It was called **Jugglers**, she said, and her father told her it was because there had been a gallows in it (a piece of black humour if ever there was one). Blackford says, rather more soberly, that a man had once been found hanging from a tree which, he says, had since been cut down.

From now on you should catch glimpses of the White Horse, at a distance as it was meant to be seen, and not close to as you saw it earlier.

The path is uneven, and the walking slightly awkward, but as you continue it improves (with occasional lapses!). The next village on the walk, Yatesbury, was, before the days of tarmac, notorious for the state of its lanes, particularly in winter. The condition of the track, you may feel, suggests that it should keep its reputation. After nearly a kilometre (½ mile), at the top of the hill, you meet another track joining yours from the left; keep on, passing a brick pillbox on the right, and 300m later again keep ahead when a further track goes off to the left. You are now passing some rather ugly old Ministry of Defence buildings (on your right), a relic of RAF Yatesbury.

The camp opened first in 1916 as a training station, but closed again in 1919. Two of the hangars from this period still survive. Although closed, the airfield remained intact, and in 1935 it was purchased by the **Bristol Aeroplane Company**, refurbished and opened as an RAF Reserve Training School. The weather that had earnt Yatesbury its bad reputation in the past delayed the opening but it was ready by April 1936. It was at this time that the third remaining hangar was built; it is now used by a haulage company. By the end of 1938 there was a Civil Air Navigation School and an Electrical and Wireless School, all housed in a large hutted camp, infamous for its bleakness in winter and its dustiness in summer.

Eventually, the demands of the wireless school as it expanded meant that the other units were forced out. During the Second World War it was so successful at training wireless operators, the camp had almost more than they knew what to do with. After the war the camp remained in use: in 1956, part of the emergency force for the Suez invasion gathered here. The station finally closed in 1969, by which time the area was designated part of the North Wessex Downs Area of Outstanding Natural Beauty. The Ministry of Defence was persuaded to remove the huts, but this left the concrete foundations. Wiltshire County Council decided the best way to 'rehabilitate' the airfield and restore it to farmland was to purchase it and bulldoze out the concrete blocks, which was mostly achieved successfully. However, one of the owners refused to sell, with the result that some buildings still survive. As you cross the fields later on, the sharp-eyed among you may notice other reminders of the RAF presence.

After a further 450m, the track meets the old approach road for the airfield. Go ahead onto this road (passing the concrete pillbox on your left) and follow it for 400m to the corner of a public road, keeping two large hangers on your right. At the corner (which appears more like a crossroads) go straight ahead towards the small village of Yatesbury. The road you are on is the only access to the village, but you are still unlikely to be disturbed by much traffic. You pass The Old Rectory (an imposing example of its type) and then the church (initially half-hidden, but very fine as you near it). After the church you pass two minor road junctions on the left; the second is called Back Lane, and leads to Manor Farm.

Yatesbury has two barrows of its own, though they are rather indistinct; one now has a water tank on it, which you may notice up to your left just after you pass Back Lane, and the other will be on your left when you start to cross the fields. More obvious perhaps are the aircraft remains just west (left) of **Manor Farm**, which you can easily see more closely by diverting along **Back Lane** for a short distance.

About 75m after passing Back Lane (800m or half a mile from the corner) turn R and take the clear track, initially with a hedge on both sides. (There is a Public Bridleway sign here, pointing to Avebury and Windmill Hill, but it can be obscured by trees. The track is immediately before the first house, a bungalow, on the right of the road.) At this point you are 11 km, 6¾ miles and 3 hours from Bishops Cannings, at GR 066714.

Proceed along this track, which is broadly straight but with a few kinks and, later, a curve to the L, for just over 1½ km (1 mile) to some trees. Shortly before these trees there is a concrete track crossing your path, a further remnant of the old airfield; you should not be tempted to trespass onto this track. At the trees, turn R and go gently uphill, on a track which is surfaced in part, for 800m (½ mile) back to the A4. The lay-by where you left your car is now only 650m on your L, and you can walk back along the wide verge if you wish. Rather pleasanter is to cross the road (the trees here are known as Cooks Plantation) and take the track opposite for 200m up onto the ridge [this short stretch of track is not a Right of Way but there seems to be no objection to its use], where you meet the outward route at the point where you came through a gap in the bank. Go through the gap, turn L (staying close to the bank) and follow the track for 650m through the clump of trees and back down to your car (14½ km, 9 miles and 4 hours from Bishops Cannings by the full route.)

For the short cut mentioned above, which starts just before the main route reaches the A4, the following notes may help. At the two barns, turn R to follow a clear track, gently uphill, between hedges on either side. After about 500m you come to a National Trust sign indicating the entry to Cherhill Down. Cross the stile and follow the track which climbs slowly, initially with a hedge and fence on the left though soon it veers away from them. As the track levels out you see a small copse ahead; here the track fades away. Keep ahead. It is not important which side of the copse you go, but if you keep to its left you will get the better view of the White Horse. Past the copse, walk towards some gates. It appears that there is a track ahead leading to the monument; but when you near the gates it is easier not to go through any of them, but to bear to the R and follow another clear track which then curves L round the nearby hillock and brings you through another gate and up to the plinth of the monument.

Go past the monument and ahead to follow the same track across the top of Oldbury Castle that you took when you departed from it this morning. Go through the gap at the far side, and bear R as before; but now, follow the track when it turns sharp L. Continue ahead and downhill; this is the track you used this morning, and you will quickly come to the gate near which you left it. Go on down to the next gate by the barns, where you bear L; then turn R at the junction about 175m further on. Follow the track back past the bomb crater, and the slight kink to R and L through the bank, to the stand of beech trees, from where the starting point is less than 400m further on. (By the short cut it is 11½ km, 7¼ miles and 3¼ hours from Bishops Cannings.)

The Country Code

Guard against all risk of fire

Every year costly damage is done by fire to crops, plantations, woodlands and heaths. Picnic fires not properly put out are one cause. A cigarette thrown away or a pipe knocked out can start a raging inferno. Be careful - a spark may do terrible damage and destroy a lifetime's work.

Fasten all gates

Animals, if they stray, can do great damage to crops and themselves. Wandering animals are a menace to themselves and others on country roads. Even if you find a gate open, always shut it behind you.

Keep your dogs under control

It is natural for a dog to chase anything that will run. Keep your dog out of temptation's way. Animals are easily frightened and the chasing of a ewe or cow may result in loss of young. When near animals or walking along the road, keep your dog on a lead.

Keep to public paths across farmland

Crops are damaged by treading, at any stage of growth. Patches of flattened corn make it difficult to harvest. Grass is also a valuable crop, remember. So please walk in single file where a path crosses a field. This keeps the path well defined and saves the crops on either side.

Use gates and stiles to cross fences, hedges and walls

If you force your way through a fence or hedge, you will weaken it. Where a person has gone an animal may follow. Stones dislodged from walls may injure people and animals, and damage crops and machinery.

Take your litter home

All litter is unsightly. Broken glass, tins and plastic bags are dangerous. They may also damage costly machinery and hold up work which it is vital to finish while the weather lasts. So leave no litter or picnic remains.

Help to keep all water clean

Water is precious in the country. Never wash dishes or bathe in somebody's water supply or foul it in any other way, or interfere with water-troughs set for cattle.

Protect wildlife, plants and trees

Wild flowers give more pleasure to more people if left to grow. Plants should never be uprooted. Trees are valuable as well as beautiful: if they are damaged their health and beauty are harmed. Birds and their eggs, animals, plants and trees should be left alone.

Take special care on country roads

Drive carefully. Blind corners, hump-backed bridges, slow-moving farm machinery and led or driven animals are all hazards for the motorist. Walk carefully too. It is generally safer to walk on the right, facing oncoming traffic.

Respect the life of the countryside

The life of the countryside centres on its work. While you are there try to fit in. Country people have to leave their belongings in the country, roads and paths run through their places of work, and you are on trust. Their work often involves hard labour. They keep early hours. So make as little noise as possible when you pass through villages in the evening. Be considerate, leave things alone, and so repay the local people for the pleasure their countryside has given you.

Before the Roman came to Rye or out to Severn strode,
The rolling English drunkard made the rolling English road.
A reeling road, a rolling road, that rambles round the shire,
And after him the parson ran, the sexton and the squire;
A merry road, a mazy road, and such as we did tread
The night we went to Birmingham by way of Beachy Head.

(from The Rolling English Road *by G.K.Chesterton)*